GRANDMA SERIES

VOLUME I

A MEMOIR

LYDIA BONGCARON WADE

authorHOUSE®

AuthorHouse™
1663 Liberty Drive
Bloomington, IN 47403
www.authorhouse.com
Phone: 1-800-839-8640

Published by AuthorHouse   10/22/2012

ISBN: 978-1-4772-5722-7 (sc)
ISBN: 978-1-4772-5721-0 (e)

Library of Congress Control Number: 2012914207

This book is printed on acid-free paper.

To my grandchildren: Stephanie, Alexandra, Gabriella, Olivia, Brian, and to the coming ones. May they appreciate their grandmother's past hard life, compare and enjoy fully the comforts of present day living . . .

ACKNOWLEDGMENTS

I am indebted to the following in the successful completion of this book:

Jerilyn Miripol, my editor, for her useful comments and corrections.

Anthony Ross, Authorhouse Publishing Consultant, for his expert advice.

Amanda M. Warren, AuthorHouse Check-in Coordinator, for her valuable assistance in the submission process,

Ann Minoza, AuthorHouse Design Consultant, for her patience and diligence during the production design process,

Renelyn Gonzales, for her help in the online submission of the manuscript; and for

Bing and Ariel Robancho, for their ever-ready assistance and support.

INTRODUCTION

GRANDMA NENE RUSHES TO THE front door when she hears a car stopping in front of her home, a James model, situated on a corner lot in Neighborhood 31 at Del Webb, Sun City. Voices familiar to her, young, excited voices, shatter the quietness of her street this hot, mid-afternoon in early July. Looking through the storm door screen, she sees her two granddaughters: Stephanie aged 12, and her sister Alexandra, 9, jump out of a black Mercedes and head towards the front entrance of the house, one trying to outrun the other.

Before she can fully open her storm door, the two girls bounce forward at the same time almost knocking her down." Hi! Grandma!" They hug her enthusiastically, speaking simultaneously.

"Welcome! Welcome!" grandma hugs them back happily, but then she notices the two dogs close behind her. "Watch out! The dogs are trying to get out!" Buddy, a white three-year old male Terrier (mixed) and Tinsel, a two and a half year old tri-colored female Beagle are close to her heels, appearing as excited as the girls. Normally, Buddy barks at people but now he just makes small yelps and wags his tail vigorously as if to say "welcome" too. Tinsel, the high-spirited one is halfway through the door but is caught in time by Clyde, her third out of three grown-up children, and father of the two girls. Behind him grinning broadly is Angela, his wife, who is heavy with child.

"How are you, mom?" Both take turns in giving her a hug. Everybody troops inside the house while Clyde heads back to the car to unload two medium-size suitcases. The children are staying with their grandma for two weeks, then they will move on with their aunt Bing and uncle Ariel in Northbridge, fifteen minutes from Del Webb, where they will spend a week. The rest of their summer will be spent with their father and his wife in Naperville.

Every summer, Stephanie and Alexandra spend their vacation in Illinois. They live with their mother, Mari, who was divorced from their father five years ago, in

Miami, Florida. These yearly vacations are always a treat for the young girls and happy times for their grandma who lives alone in this large retirement community, south of downtown Chicago.

It is now 4:30 in the afternoon, oppressively hot and humid. The group had started out from Naperville at 2:00 p.m. "You must be hungry. I have prepared home-made pizza and lemonade." Grandma hurries to her small kitchen and brings out a freshly baked cheese pizza into the dining area. In-between bites of pizza and gulps of the cool drink, the two girls chatter about their camp experiences in Miami before they left for Chicago. The barking of Buddy trying to get attention does not deter their chattering. Sometimes they speak at the same time prompting their daddy to intervene.

"What do you plan to do with the children during the coming two weeks, mom?" Clyde inquires as he finishes his third slice of pizza.

"Oh, there's so much for them to do, watch and see," grandma replies, smiling at the two kids. "Stephanie can continue her tennis lessons she started last year, Angela puts in. We saw a group of children playing tennis at the Tall Oaks Tennis court on our way here".

"I'll see if Tom, the tennis instructor, has a spot for her this year. Turning to Alexandra, she says: "What about you sweetie, would you like to join your sister?"

"No, grandma, I would rather go swimming. You ought to see the two swimming pools at the Prairie Lodge, daddy. One is indoor and is bigger, the other one, outdoor is beautiful, surrounded with well-trimmed shrubs and different flowers. Oh, I'd love to make a splash in the pool right now! Wouldn't you too, Stephanie?" "I sure do", is the sister's brief answer, munching her pizza.

"Here's the plan", grandma begins as she sits in her recliner after the hearty snacks and when everybody is settled in the living area. This coming two weeks will be short to fit in all the things I have in mind for the girls. Stephanie has shown interest in food preparation and cooking." At this, she gets Stephanie's full attention from petting Tinsel. I have selected a number of recipes from my collection that are easy and simple, mostly snacks and dessert recipes.

"Are you also interested in cooking, Alexandra?" her daddy asks. "No, thanks. But I will help in the clearing up", she smiles demurely at everybody.

"I bet you will help a lot in the "practical evaluation", Angela says laughing.

"We shall be busy, very busy, indeed", grandma continues. We shall be doing those we did not do last summer, and the summer before it.

"Is shopping at the mall included, grandma?" Stephanie wants to know. "Of course, as always. There is a new Wal-

Mart store close to Del Webb, about four miles from here. There are yet a number of outlets we had not been to before on Randall Road."

"Hmm, get your checkbook and credit cards ready, mom", says her son. "It will be my pleasure, dear. After all, they are with me only once in a year. I wish their cousin Gabriella were here also. Let's see if she can join you next year." Oh, incidentally, there is something I have thought of doing with you which we had not done before."

"What is it, grandma?" Alexandra asks anxiously as she moves over to grandma's side.

"The last two years you had been coming here, we had spent our evenings watching DVD movies. You had exhausted your uncle Ariel's DVD collection as well as mine. I have bought new ones from Blockbuster and Borders, but this time, we shall alternate our evening entertainment between watching movies and storytelling."

"Storytelling! Alexandra interjects. I love storytelling! I have not heard bedtime stories in a long time. We always have a lot of homework in the evening, and by the time we finish, it is time to sleep. Most times we are not able to watch our favorite shows anymore."

"That's true, grandma. I am excited to hear your stories for a change. Who knows I can get ideas for my own stories one day?" Stephanie joins her grandma and sister. Both sit on either side of the reclining chair. "Stephanie has an ambition to become a writer one day, mom", Clyde says smiling. She has a big collection of short stories and novels at home in Miami. Stephanie, your grandma's stories should be a good resource for you, dear."

"I think you girls are too old for fantasy tales about prince and princesses, about goblins and enchanted castles and of dark knights. Instead, you will hear about authentic real-life stories which I myself had experienced during my childhood days in our old, sleepy town, south of the Philippine Islands." Grandma stands up and takes a calendar made of cloth with a colored map of the Philippines which hangs on a wall in her small corridor. "Here, this is where your grandma was born and grew up", she points the spot to her curious grandchildren.

"Have you been to this place, daddy?" "No, not yet. Maybe someday," their daddy responds with a grin.

"Maybe after you hear my stories, you all might want to go there," grandma says looking from one to the other. "Wow! That would really be interesting. I would like to hear those stories myself," says Angela, caught in the moment's enthusiasm.

"Well, but you won't my dear. Right now, we should be preparing to leave. You are on call tonight at St. Francis Hospital, remember?" Clyde takes his wife by the hand, and facing the children, addresses them. "Girls, listen carefully to your grandma's stories as we will be asking you to re-tell them when you are back with us. "How's your new hospital, dear?" Nene asks Angelina as she follows the two towards the door. "Oh, I am the newest pediatrician in this hospital It is closer home. It is only five minutes away and I can come home for lunch."

"Mom, don't you think the girls would be bored with your stories?" Clyde says as they are leaving. "Daddy, we like to hear true stories, not fiction", says Stephanie seriously.

"What's fiction, Stephanie?" Alexandra wants to know. "Fiction is a story based on imaginary characters and situations. It is the opposite of a true story," grandma explains.

"We shall see you girls in two weeks", the father says as they wave goodbye. Following their grandma into the kitchen, the two girls take one more slice of pizza each.

"You have to teach me how to make pizza, grandma," Stephanie says in between bites of the thin-crusted pastry. "What about if we sell pizza and lemonade in front of your house, grandma? I see a lot of cars passing by your street."

"Girls in our neighborhood in Miami sell cold drinks during the summer. Can we do that here?" Alexandra reinforces her sister's suggestion.

"Oh no! We are not allowed to do that here. Besides, who will do all the squeezing of the lemons?" grandma replies smiling at her grandchildren.

Grandma ushers the two girls to the living room and takes out a DVD which she knows they will enjoy watching, a dog story entitled, "Far From Home, Yellow Dog." Enjoy the movie you two while I make soup and salad for dinner. We just had a heavy and late snack. What we need for dinner is something light. I made a really delicious dessert, "Leche Flan", your father's favorite. I should have given him some, but I forgot."

"I thought you were going to tell us your stories, grandma?" Stephanie inquires as grandma is about to put on the movie. I am more keen on hearing them, than watching a movie."

"Not today, sweetheart. We shall start the storytelling tomorrow night. I have mail to open, and a few phone calls to make now. And this evening, Mr. Wright is coming to do Backflow Prevention Test."

"What's that about, grandma?" Alexandra, the ever-inquisitive one asks. "It is a test done every year, to ensure the free flow of water through the pipes in case of fire."

I

LIFE IN A FARM—WORLD WAR II, 1943

WE LIVED IN THE MIDDLE of a large farm situated about 2 kilometers from the heart of Lopez Jaena, one of the smallest towns in the province of Misamis Occidental in Mindanao, south of the Philippines. My family consisted of my father, mother, one brother, my four sisters and I. I was the youngest in the family and when World War II broke out, I was only about 3 years old.

My father was a policeman and my mother was a full time housewife, saddled with the duties of looking after six young children and minding the farm. We had two dozen or so chickens, five pigs, a carabao (buffalo-like animal), which was used a lot in plowing our rice field and farm land, and four dogs. Each member of the family no matter how young had duties to perform. I was taught how to feed the chickens in my young age. Nobody was allowed to be idle.

My brother and sisters were roused from bed at sunrise even during the weekends when there was no school. I had a few concessions being the smallest, and was exempted from fetching water from the spring. Our house was on a hill, and to get to the spring, one had to climb down a rugged and stony path, and climb up again to where the spring was at the crest of another hill. The spring water had to be scooped from the well with a dipper and into a bamboo pole hacked inside to hold the water. The job was too much for me to do.

My older sister, Mary, (May she rest in peace) the third from the oldest was my favorite. Whenever she would fetch water from the spring, I would tag along. She would carry me on her back while carrying the bamboo pole full of water on her shoulder. I was a naughty, spoiled brat. Most times, I would cry if I did not get what I wanted, and the one who caused me to cry got some pinching from my mother. She was a disciplinarian but very loving and caring. God rest her soul.

During the war, our province was overrun by the Japanese. My brother who was seventeen years old joined the USAFFE, so did my two uncles from my mother's side. The acceptable age to join the army was eighteen but my brother lied about his age. Being very tall for his age, he was accepted into the Medical team in the USAFFE.

"What is the meaning of USAFFE, grandma?" Alexandra cuts in for the first time. "United States Armed Forces in the Far East." Seeing the opportunity to interrupt, Stephanie speaks rapidly. "You said you had a big farm. What did you plant, and what did you do to help?"

"Good question, dear. We had a lot of bananas, corn, cassava, pineapples, peanuts and sweet potatoes. Around our house were varieties of mangoes, jackfruit, avocados, guyabanos, guavas and lanzones. Many of these local fruits are not known here in the U.S."

We also had a big rice field in the valley where a river flowed alongside it. Our whole farm was full of coconut trees from end to end. The coconut by-product we called copra was a good source of income for us. In fact, our school tuition fees and other expenses were paid for by our income from copra. Copra was produced by drying coconut meat until crisp. They were put in brown sacks, tied up and then sold by the kilo. Each kilo would cost from 10 to 15 centavos.

We were living in abundance of food supply, thanks to the hard work of my family especially my father and mother. I did very little as I was young then. The most I could do was feed and play with the dogs; and yes, munch on those juicy sugar canes that bordered the farm. When my mother was working in the farm, she would call me occasionally to bring her water to drink from an earthen jar in one corner of the shed. Sometimes I would pick guavas and then sleep in a hammock hanging in the shed.

Many of the town folk would come to our place to barter corn or bananas with fresh fish or seashells. My mother was so generous she would give other things like preserved pineapples or mangoes she made herself, ripe jackfruit and other ripe fruits which we could not consume by ourselves. Both my parents were well loved by the townspeople not only because of their friendliness but also because of their generosity. Perhaps this was the reason why one day at the height of the Japanese occupation, a group of five families came to our place from another town to settle in our farm. They were called "Evacuees". The head of the group was the wife of a prominent Muslim businessman who was killed by the Japanese at the start of the occupation.

The woman's name was Dashinag. She was very beautiful with flowing hair, fair complexion, tall and slender, with shapely long legs. She was about 34 years old. She had four young children who were very shy. I could not forget how the little one obviously the youngest, about my age and a girl, cried so hard when I touched her long hair. The children were constantly tugging at their mother's skirt.

The rest of the evacuees would bow to the woman before they spoke to her and withdrew with bowed heads. My mother told us that Dashinag was the daughter of a royal Muslim couple from Zamboanga del Norte. She was then a princess. We should show respect for her at all times, she emphasized. Some evacuees settled in other remote parts of our province, coming from places occupied by the Japanese. "Wait grandma, what are evacuees?" Stephanie anxiously asks. "I have never come across that word before in my readings."

"Evacuees are people running away or leaving their homes to escape some disaster like war, disease or other calamities. Our place was ideal for hiding. There were rows of coconut trees and fruit trees around our farm house which almost entirely hid it from view.

At the back of our house was a slope leading to the valley below with a river running through, snaking along a wide rice field. Bamboo trees, more fruit trees, coconuts and shrubs of all types abound all over the area. Across the valley lie a steep hill doted with more coconut trees. The area where the evacuees settled was a perfect hideaway."

They built nipa huts along the river. There must had been ten huts housing about two dozen people, excluding children. "Grandma," Alexandra tugs at grandma's arm. "What are nipa huts?"

"They are tiny houses made of bamboo and nipa, type of palm trees that grow in the swamps. They have sturdy leaves ideal for roofing. Bamboos are tall, graceful trees that bend in the wind but have strong and tough trunks. These two trees were common materials for building houses and huts during my time. Even today, they are still used along with wood and aluminum."

For the princess and her four children and two maids, they built the largest hut in the middle of the compound. The family was always huddled together as if in constant fear. The lady princess wore glittering jewelry even when sleeping. The two maids attended to her every need and her children's, aged 8, 6, 4 and 3. They obviously brought ample provisions with them but occasionally she would send a message to my mother asking to borrow salt. My mother in her usual generosity would send to her not only salt but also some root crops and fruits. No sooner had they settled when the men and the younger women in the group cleared the hillsides and the vacant areas in the valley and planted corn, cassavas other root crops, bananas and more fruit trees.

One day, one of the maids came up to our house and spoke to my mother. "It is my lady's 35th birthday today, ma'am. She would like to celebrate it here in your house, if you will permit it. None of the huts down there is big enough to hold all of us at the same time."

"Of course," my mother readily gave permission. "Would she like to buy one of our pigs and some chickens perhaps?" The maid went and came back with, "My lady said, thank you so much for the offer. She and her children do not eat pork, but the rest of us do. They can have the chicken. She will send some of our people to do the preparations."

My mother and two women put out the vats (large cooking pots) and earthen jars to fill with water. Five men came to slaughter our biggest pig and six chickens. Three others joined in cleaning the slaughtered animals and in filling the earthen jars with water from the spring. They worked silently but with much enthusiasm.

By nightfall, our surroundings were filled with the aroma of cooked food. Our neighbors came, curious about the hub of activity and of the unusual number of people hovering around our place. Although uninvited, they remained to participate in the fun and in the big dinner. The cooked foods were laid out on long bamboo benches lined with banana leaves and then brought into our big dining room upstairs.

The birthday lady who came with the children and maids was smiling happily at everybody. She looked so breathtakingly beautiful with her long hair held at the nape with a large, glittering comb. Her long gown glittered with multi-colored sequins around the neckline, around her slim waist, and along the hemline. She carried a large red embroidered fan which she waved gracefully to the adoring crowd. Everybody watched her every move with silent awe.

After "Happy Birthday" was sung, she went over to my mother, kissed her on the cheek and thanked her for the elaborate celebration. My mother, a very good cook, oversaw all the food preparation. There was sampayna (made of entrails and pig blood), a favorite native dish, apritada (fricassee), adobo, menudo, asado, stuffed chicken, grilled and fried chicken and a variety of sautéed vegetables. Rice was the main accompaniment but there were also platters of sweet potatoes, boiled bananas and cassava. There were a variety of fresh fruits and a big ripe jackfruit picked from our backyard for dessert.

"Have you seen a jackfruit, Stephanie?" Instead of answering her sister, Stephanie turns to grandma inquiringly. "Jackfruit is a tropical fruit from a tree that grows from 10 to 14 ft high. The fruit is big with spikes, round or oval and weighs from four pounds to 10 or more lbs. It has sweet-smelling thick pulps with big seeds inside that could be boiled or roasted. The cooked seeds tasted like potatoes." I can still remember how we would build fire, roast the seeds and enjoyed eating them.

"Do we have this kind of fruit here, grandma? It sounds strange to me," comment from Alexandra. "Yes, it is at some Korean or Filipino stores but rare. It is also available canned or preserved. Oh, fresh ripe jackfruit is so sweet and delicious! You can smell ripe jackfruit even from a distance."

"The sumptuous dinner was served in our large dining room," grandma continues. The lady princess brought out some wine that the men took turns in tasting. We had our local wine too, called "tuba". Tuba is sap extracted from coconut and fermented. This wine is very potent and the men who drank profusely got drunk even before the music and the dancing began that night.

When my father arrived from his duty as policeman, he brought out his saxophone and played. He was accompanied by someone with a guitar. Then my oldest sister put on the phonograph, one of the items mama had inherited from my grandparents who died when I was a baby.

The people had fun watching me and the other children dancing. They threw coins at us. I collided with another child when we scrambled for the coins and developed a big bump on my forehead. Then, someone stepped on my toes. That's when I really cried.

"Poor grandma!", the two girls exclaim with giggles.

Noise and music blended together in a loud pitch as the night wore on. Kerosene lamps and candles were our sources of lighting. The almost full moon added more illumination outside. The revelers spilled onto the porch and into our spacious lawn lined with bougainvillas and gumamelas (local flowering shrubs). More tuba (coconut wine) were served. Drinking and merriment continued into the night.

Japanese Bombs! Black Out!

Way after midnight when I was on the verge of dozing off in spite of the noise, loud explosions cut into the night. Sounds of airplanes from all over filled the night.air. The coconut trees shook and swayed like graceful dancing maidens. Everybody stopped singing, dancing or drinking. Many ran out and hid underneath the house. Time seemed to stop while the explosions became louder and closer.

"Bombs! Bombs! The Japanese are coming!", someone screamed in panic. All froze in fear except me. I hastily jumped off my mama's lap and blew off the lamps and candles in one big sweep. The whole house became pitch dark and quiet as in a cave. No one dared to breath as the planes passed over our house. The strong vibrations shook the house from its foundations. Children cried and their mothers could not pacify them. I clung to my mama so tightly she had difficulty extracting my thin arms from around her neck. Papa and my sisters joined us at a corner. My dear father held his family protectively.

Everything became quiet again after moments of eminent danger. People came out from their hiding places hesitatingly, slowly recovering from fear. An old man came over to me, held my two shoulders and said in a quivering voice: "Of all the adult people in here nobody was sensible enough to observe "black out" during a raid, except this young, innocent child." Most of the crowd of people bowed in silent approval. They clapped their hands making me feel really grand. My mama kissed me and my father held me up proudly.

"You were a hero, grandma!" exclaims Stephanie. Both girls clap their hands and hug their grandma lovingly. "Please go on, grandma", says Alexandra.

A tall man spoke slowly, deliberately: "That raid was so close I thought we would be hit. They bombed Oroquieta, the capital last week. Then they concentrated on the hills and on Malindang mountain to rout out the guerrillas."

"Lord! Protect my son," mama prayed aloud. The people prayed with her except the Muslims who remained in shock. We breathed more easily as the sound of the planes faded away in the distance. No one dared to light the lamps again although the roaring of the planes had long died down. The Muslim princess appeared more terrified than the others. Her husband who was killed at the onset of the occupation was the head of a town. He was rich and influential.

The Japanese targeted not only the guerrillas but also the town heads and rich people who were suspected of supporting the guerrillas and members of the USAFFE. The enemies knew that if they captured these elite groups, it would be easier to capture the soldiers who relied on their support by way of food and influence.

Farms in the richer towns were raided of livestock, rice, corn, root crops, fowls, other food items and things, whatever they could use for their troops.

Stephanie sits up and asks anxiously, "Grandma, how about your farm? Did they not come and raid your farm too?" "That was what my parents were nervous about. If they would come to our farm, how would we survive then? Besides we were harboring a lot of evacuees consisting of strong, able men. They could easily have suspected them as guerrillas."

"Oh dear!" Alexandra cups her small face with both hands looking worried. Grandma sees she is afraid to hear more of the ensuing events. Grandma's next account eases both girls' building tension. "Fortunately, of all the twelve towns in our province ours was the only town which was not invaded by the Japanese. They came only as far as Molatuhan, 40 kilometers from our town.

Mama said later that the reason why they spared our town was because my two uncles who were captured and used as interpreters, would kneel in front of the Commander whenever they would discuss to invade our small town. They would plead and say:" Let us not go to Lopez Jaena. There is nothing we can get from that poor town, and all the people had already left."

The Japanese Commander would routinely kick them and spat at them when he got annoyed with their entreaties. My uncles persevered in their pleadings nevertheless.

When the war was over, some U.S. soldiers and their Filipino counter parts (USAFFE) came into town signaling the liberation. My only brother was among them. All the townspeople came out from their hiding places jubilantly. They hugged and cheered the marching troops. Sadly, my two uncles were brought to Kolambugan, Misamis Oriental, the adjacent province to ours and were thrown into the garrison. They were accused of collaborating with the Japanese.

"There are two words I should like you to explain, grandma," Stephanie says at the end of the evening's narrative. "What is meant by "garrison" and "collaborating?"

A garrison is a fort, a place where soldiers get imprisoned and kept indefinitely until they are tried and released, or maybe killed. In those days life was never certain. "Collaborating means cooperating or helping the enemy. We lived in fear for our two uncles' lives as they were kept in the garrison for as long as I could remember.

"Know what girls? I like your inquisitiveness. That is a sign of mental alertness.". Grandma ruffles the girls' long hair as she straightens up from the couch.

"You should have your hair cut, shoulder length at least. Long hair is harder to maintain, don't you think?"

"Oh no, grandma. We like it this way. Most girls in my class have long hair. It's the style. Stephanie's younger sister nods in agreement.

"Goodnight, girls". Grandma kisses each of the girls and tucks them in.

II

A TRIP TO THE GARRISON

I MUST HAVE BEEN FIVE or six years old after the Liberation, when I went with mother, my oldest sister and my mother's two younger brothers on a voyage to Kolambugan, Misamis Oriental, about two days by sailboat from our shores. We were bound for the garrison situated close to the seashore to visit my two other uncles who were imprisoned there. My mother did not want to take me with them but I cried endlessly until she relented, but only after giving me the most painful pinch on my buttocks. Hearing this, the two grandchildren roar with laughter.

I remember very clearly the day when we set sail at daybreak on a large sailboat with bamboo balances on each side (katig). In the middle hoisted high were two white tarpaulin sails swaying in the gentle breeze. The sky was clear blue and I could see seagulls flirting with one another, circling the sky directly above us. The sun was just beginning to rise when we pulled off from an old, decaying platform often used by fishermen. My uncles Jose and Joshua manned the boat, one in front of the other using big paddles made out of thick wood. The sailboat had an engine but gas was rare and expensive so they used it sparingly. They rowed most of the time taking turns to rest.

The oars made splashy, swishy noises as they hit the water. The bamboo balances (katig) would groan and squeak like they did not want to go. Apart from these noises it was otherwise a calm, peaceful sailing on a sunny morning along the smooth, aquamarine waters off the coast of our province.

My mother laid out layers of blankets on the bamboo bench in the middle of the boat for me to lie down. It was big and wide enough for my oldest sister and me. I slept like a baby until the bright sun hit my forehead and arms. I realized it was now midday. My mother and my sister were at the other end of the boat preparing a meal on a makeshift stove with live coal. My uncles dropped anchor and we ate our lunch under the shade of the wide sails. It was fun to eat in the middle of the ocean, like we were having a picnic.

The evening became very chilly and I slept fitfully. I dreamed of a sea monster about to devour me had it been for an old man who grabbed me on time. "Oh, grandma!" both girls exclaim. "That's more like a horror story!" says Stephanie. "It was, in my dream of course," grandma says with a chuckle.

We arrived at the fort the following day about mid-afternoon. We trooped towards the garrison led by my mother. I clung to my mother's skirt while the others followed right behind us.

My mother spoke to the uniformed officer at the entrance to a walled enclosure. It took a while for us to get passes to the garrison. Another officer, an older man, spoke to my mother partly in Cebuano and partly in English. He finally signaled to a passing soldier asking him to take us to an inner gate. A few uniformed men with armbands presumably guards, eyed us curiously. We must have been quite a sight with our partly wet clothes and unkempt hair. We did not have the chance to change clothes as my mother was in a rush to see our prisoner uncles before the gates were closed to visitors. The sign at the entrance that prompted us to hurry, said: "No Visitors Allowed After Five."

We were not permitted to enter the garrison itself. We were told to wait behind a square window with steel bars. The bars could be opened to allow the prisoners to kiss or hug their visiting family members or friends. My mother cried when she saw her brothers. Their prison clothes looked like they had not been washed in ages.

I was very young when they joined the army so I did not recognize them. Uncle Peter and Uncle Roman hugged each one of my two younger uncles, my sister and then my mother, who did not want to release them from her embrace. When it was my turn, my mother held me up so that they could kiss me. I shuddered from the coarseness of their beard on my skin as they took turns in kissing and hugging me.

"Nene, (as I was called then) how big you have grown!" my uncle Peter remarked, eyeing me through and through with tears in his eyes. My uncle Roman pinched me on my cheek so hard I winced.

"Did you bring us something to eat from home?" Uncle Peter peered into the basket my older sister was holding. "Oh yes, yes," my mother said, taking the basket from my sister. We brought you grilled fish (bulad), boiled saba bananas and sweet potatoes, fresh ripe bananas and peanuts, all from the farm, except the fish, of course. They grabbed the basket gleefully.

"These are a treat," said uncle Roman, rummaging through the goodies. We have not eaten these in a long time. They give us boiled corn meal and canned vegetables most of the time and occasional corned beef (carne norte). Fruits are served once a week only, on Sundays. We are not really starving, but we long for our home food. The U.S. officers are kinder to us and give us bigger servings than our own men. Our own soldiers still think we have betrayed our own people."

"When are you going to be released? It had been two years since you were brought here," my mother asked anxiously. "Maybe a year or two more. We have no idea exactly."

"Maybe we should speak to the garrison commander?" Uncle Jose suggested. "It seems that they are waiting for a high official from the U.S. Armed Forces who will make decisions about our fate." Uncle Peter said. "They had been saying that for weeks. I won't believe in anything they say until I see it happen." Uncle Roman commented wryly.

"I will speak to the Governor, my second degree cousin, if he could do something to speed up your release," Mama promised. After a tearful goodbye, we trooped back to the seashore where our boat was moored and took a black bag containing our clothes. My mother, my sister and I headed to the home of my mother's friend in town, the wife of a Chinese, who recently opened a variety store along the road to the pier. We slept in a cramped attic room with a tiny window overlooking the sea. My two uncles Jose and Joshua remained in the boat. They would not leave the boat overnight unattended lest we would find ourselves without transportation back home the next day.

We saw our garrisoned uncles again before we left the following day. The day looked gloomy and the breeze felt cold and wet. The sky was gray and small intermittent drops of rain fell into the seawater forming tiny ripples. The gentle breeze turned into gusts. The sea gulls flew in a frenzy as if chased by an unforeseen force. My uncles hesitated and suggested we stay another day as the weather did not seem ideal for a sea voyage, but my mother would not hear of it.

"Let us go now and head for the nearest town across the channel before the rainstorm takes head. It does not look ominous to me, probably just a passing rain like three days ago," she declared confidently. She wanted to hurry back and resume work in the farm. Her paid workers were waiting for her. It was time for planting corn, and the coconuts were ready for harvesting again after three months interval. My mother being older made the decisions. My uncles had little to say about matters of importance.

All through the afternoon, my sister and I slept after lunch of cold rice and salted fish. My mother helped in adjusting and shifting the sail while my uncles rowed vigorously amid the mounting waves. It was dark when I awoke from the loud clapping of thunder. My uncles were quiet in their task maneuvering the boat over the rough seas. My mother could not hide her nervousness seeing the giant waves threatening our hapless boat.

"Joshua, move over to the other side of the boat!", she ordererd with urgency. The rain was falling in big drops creating slouchy sounds as it hit the turbulent waters. Lightning pierced the sky in rapid succession followed by deafening thunder. From the light brought by the lightning which came seemingly close to the tips of our sail, I could make out huge waves threatening to engulf our boat as it rolled and pitched like a roller coaster. I screamed and screamed in horror.

"Get down! Get down! Lie on your stomach!" I heard my mother's shrill voice above the storm. "Meding, help me bail out!" she turned to my sister who was crouching behind me, trembling in fear.

Reluctantly, she joined my mother and soon both worked feverishly to rid the hold of the boat with water which filled in as quickly as it was bailed out.

Uncle Jose tried to work the engine but it sounded weak and would stop right after it started. He cursed while my uncle Joshua, his younger brother, uttered a prayer loudly. "Jesus, we are in the middle of a big storm, help us!" My mother grew quiet and still. I knew she was also praying. I was crying hysterically. My sister stopped bailing out and hugged me while I was lying face down. I was soaked, she was soaked, everybody was soaked and trembling in the cold. The boat continued to rock from side to side, up and down endlessly. I was throwing up and my sister was also throwing up. When I moved to shift my position, I lost my grip of the side of the boat and tumbled into the angry sea, flailing like a loose leaf.

"Grandma!" The girls scream in unison. Alexandra covers her face with her two hands and Stephanie clutches her grandma's arm in fear. Grandma is silent for a second, as if re-living her ordeal. Heaving a deep sigh, she continues:

"Nene!" my mother screamed, as she was trying to catch me. I could not swim of course, and I immediately swallowed a lot of seawater. Uncle Jose dove after me and grabbed my arm as I began to sink. My mother and sister helped hoist me back into the hold of the boat. I could not speak for a long while. My mother laid me upside down and patted my neck and back vigorously until the sea water came out of my mouth. I then cried aloud, trembling both from the cold and from my frightful ordeal. A blanket was put around me but it did not help much because it was saturated with water.

Everything in the boat was soaking wet. The storm was still on but by now, was lesser in intensity. The giant waves which threatened to swallow our boat, had subsided a bit. The boat had become steadier in its glide, but I dared not move although I was safely cradled in Mama's arms. "Let us try to make it to the nearest shore," I heard Mama say in a steadier voice." Which direction, left, right or straight ahead?", uncle Jose asked, obviously unable to figure out our position.

"Just go on rowing. The Lord will direct us," she said confidently. We should hit Aloran shores if we continue on our present course." Aloran is a town east of Lopez Jaena, some fifty or so kilometers from our municipality. Like our town, Aloran is a coastal municipality next to the capital, Oroquieta.

After what seemed a lifetime of cold, misery and fear, we finally hit solid ground. I was shivering more from the cold now, than from fear. Danger from the horrible storm in the middle of the deepest ocean between our province and Misamis Oriental was over now." Grandma pauses as she observes the girls' look of relief. Oh thank God!" Alexandra sighs, while Stephanie's' face clears with her usual sweet smile. "What a frightful story, grandma!".

The feel of the sandy shore on our bare feet was very comforting. My mother knelt down on the dry sand and said her prayer of thanks. My sister kissed the jotting stone nearby, while I kicked the white sand playfully with my small bare feet, sending a cloud of the white stuff in the air. On the other hand, my two uncles struggled to push the boat and tied it safely on a huge driftwood lying close to the seashore.

Some good-hearted fishermen family who lived not very far from where we anchored took us for the night in their shabby little nipa hut, and provided us with some dry clothing and ragged blankets. I was so cold I did not mind wearing an old, oversized dress which hang around my small, thin frame. I must have looked like a scarecrow. Picturing a scarecrow, both girls laugh heartily. The blankets were old too and in tatters. Worse, it smelled of a cat's urine, but I did not mind that either. "He! He!" Stephanie and Alexandra are now giggling out of control. Grandma joins the girls' contagious mirth.

The head of the family of five who gave us sanctuary solemnly remarked, "It was a miracle you did not capsize, thank the Lord! That was a very bad storm, the worst we ever had this year, so far." By then the rain had completely abated, and the pale moon had emerged from the sky which an hour ago was very dark and menacing.

In her gratefulness, my mother offered the last of our provisions of dried fish and bananas to the family the following morning before we started out on the last leg of our voyage home. The family did not seem to have much by way of food and other necessities but bountiful in their hospitality and kindness.

III

THE ROLLING MONSTER

A COUPLE OF MONTHS AFTER that frightening episode at sea on our return journey from the garrison in Kolambugan, Misamis Oriental, my mother decided that I should now start school. My other older sister, the third from our oldest, Manding Mary, as we younger siblings addressed her with respect, took me to the town two kilometers away from our farm, to enroll me in Grade I. "Excuse me, grandma, did you not say you were only about five or six years old? Shouldn't you have been in Kindergarten?" "No, sweetheart, in those days, there was no kindergarten. We went straight to grade school" grandma smiles at Stephanie's inquiry.

I was thin, very shy and ignorant too. Although my mother would tell us bedtime stories about Cinderella, Sinbad the Sailor, Hansel and Gretel, The Seven Dwarfs, stories of witches and enchanted castles, I was not yet exposed to the classroom and listening and learning with a group. I had not the slightest idea about school. My sister told me that it was fun but you had better pay attention all the time to the teacher or you get whacked with a stick. The thought frightened me. She also said that this teacher person would ask a lot of questions and if you don't speak she or he would let you stand in front of all the other pupils throughout the class. She would tell you what to do and what not to do like she was your mother.

He or she would sing and dance with you, do exercises and many other things besides. Now the mention of singing and dancing made me happy, at least temporarily. I loved to sing and dance. I still do. "Do you like singing and dancing girls?" she asks. "I like to watch, but I feel awkward dancing," says Stephanie. "Same here, grandma, but I like singing," says Alexandra showing her dimple as she smiles. "It is alright. Some skills can be developed later. Exposure to certain skills helps a lot. We shall discuss these topics next time. In the meantime, would you girls like me to continue this story? It is kind of funny, you know." "Sure, grandma!" the two girls settle more closely to grandma on the couch.

My teacher turned out to be very gentle and kind. She was tall and slim and had a ready smile for everyone. I liked her instantly and listened to every word she had to say with rapt attention. Everything seems new and strange to me. On my second day, the girl next to me cried asking for her mother. The other girl next to her had pinched her arm. During recess time, somebody stole my snack, two small boiled bananas. Then, before we were sent home for the day, one of the boys in my class fell through the window when he was leaning out to call a friend. And worst for me, I stumbled into a garden plot fenced around with bamboo sticks. My right knee got scratched badly. I was bleeding and the school nurse was called. My sister Mary had to carry me home that day. I felt sorry for her but I felt so much pain each time I would try to walk. I did not go to school again until the following week.

At the end of my third day in school, while my sister and I were heading back home, she remembered that Mama had asked her to do an errand for her in town, so we had to go back to the center of the town where the stores were. It must have been about 5:00 in the afternoon.

While we were walking on one side of the street, I saw to my amazement what looked like a monster with two large eyes, rolling down the street noisily towards us. When it was closing in on us, I screamed! I was so terrified my sister could not keep me from running down the street away from the "monster." While the thing was coming closer and closer, I ran zigzag, screaming harder and harder as I went, like a mad person. There were men on the "thing" wearing stupid round head covers (helmets actually). I kept zigzagging across the road like a trapped mouse. Meanwhile, my sister was howling behind me trying to catch up.

What I could not understand at the time was, nobody else was doing what I was doing. Were they not scared of the monster? They did not appear afraid at all. Some were even laughing! Finally, the thing stopped moving and a uniformed man, (a U.S. soldier) with the stupid green hat got off from the front of the thing and caught me in time before I could run again. "Sst! Sst! It's okay child. Don't be afraid. This is only a jeep. Not a monster to eat you up," the man said, holding me on both shoulders. He was grinning at me, his blue eyes looking at me with amusement, his perfectly white teeth showing from a well-shaped mouth. The two other soldiers inside the vehicle were grinning too.

"Oh grandma!" Alexandra cannot suppress a laugh. But Stephanie says seriously, "Grandma was so scared Alexandra. You would be too, if you were in her position." She adds reproachfully.

One of the men seated in the back tossed a candy bar which landed on my feet, and the third man, seated with the driver in the front seat with medals hanging on his breast pocket, beckoned to me to come to him. "You are so cute, child. I have a daughter back in America. She was five years old when I left." He stopped briefly to recollect. "About three years ago. How old are you, kid?"

"She is six years old, sir." My sister caught up and answered the question, which I found hard to understand. He spoke differently and rapidly. I knew he was speaking in English, for I heard my teacher speaking it with other teachers. But this man, an officer in the U.S. Army spoke in a strange sort of way (slang). "Sorry, sir, first time she see jeep!" my sister apologized in crooked English.

My sister was only in Grade Five then, but at least she could manage a little of the foreign language. The officer took out a box of candy and gave it to me. He gave another one to my sister. "Thank you, sir. Say 'Thank you'" she urged me.

When the soldiers had left in their jeep, I cried, not in fear anymore, but of shame. People gathered around us and saw that my sister gave me a pinch on my ear lobe.

"Don't be too hard on the child!" said one elderly person. She was genuinely terrified. "What do you expect? She never saw a jeep before, did she?" The small group of people around us were obviously amused by the whole episode. One openly laughed aloud and was joined by the rest. Stephanie is now laughing hard with Alexandra. They laugh so loud that Tinsel and Buddy who were sleeping at the foot of the couch wake up in wonder.

"Oh, grandma! That was really funny! I wish somebody could have taken a picture of you!" Stephanie is trying to stifle another laugh.

"It was not funny for me at the time, girls. The thing scared me to death. You know, when I think of it now, I should not have been ashamed of what I had done, the innocent that I was."

I pitied my sister Mary, though. When she told the story to our mother as soon as we got home that day, she was crying. She said two of her classmates saw what happened. She bet the whole class would know the full story the following day and she would be taunted and ridiculed.

The next day, she skipped classes in spite of my mother's scolding.

IV

CHRISTMAS STORY

CHRISTMAS WAS ONE OF MY favorite holidays, as it is with most children here in the U.S. and in many Christian countries as well. Although we also got gifts, simple and cheap ones mostly from our parents, we celebrated the season a little differently.

It was customary to do caroling from the start of the Christmas season on Dec. 16th, also the start of the dawn masses. Caroling extended after Dec. 25th to Jan. 6th, The Epiphany. I belonged to a group of carolers including my two older sisters and girls from two other families. There were 8 of us in the group. I being the youngest was called the "angel". Caroling then did not only involve singing but dancing as well. Vising, a tall, vivacious young lady of 18 was our leader. We all wondered where she had learned all the dance steps and the music, but she could really dance, sing and taught us well too. Up to this day she is still alive and strong in her late eighties and from what I heard, still continues to teach children in my town how to dance, bless her. I should endeavor to see her when I go home this coming November.

My group consisted of from aged 5(me) to 13. We were called "Pastores"(Shepherds) and our dances were supposed to re-enact what the shepherds did during the birth of Jesus in Bethlehem. We were all dressed in white clothes and I being the angel, had a pair of wings made of crepe paper and cardboard, attached to my back with a string. My group members would start the initial singing and dancing in the middle of the room. When they stopped, I would enter and do my own singing and dancing alone as they clap their hands to the rhythm. My song went this way in our native language: "Usa kadto ka gabiing maanyag," meaning, one evening when the moon and the stars were shining brightly, Jesus was born in a manger, etc." The family whom we were caroling used to be very delighted with me and my performance that they would throw coins at me while I was dancing. "Wow, grandma," Alexandra interrupts. "That was great!" Well, I had to turn over the money to our keeper to be included into our earnings for the night. "Why would you turn over your money?" Stephanie wants to know. "Because those were the rules," grandma calmly answers, then continues:

We would start caroling late in the afternoon and end up around 7:00 P.M. Mama forbade us from staying out late. Every house we visited gave us money and served us native fares such as bibingka (rice cakes), suman (ginger-flavored rice wrapped in banana leaves), puto (steamed ground rice) with sugar and coconut milk, and chocolate drink. We enjoyed those caroling days tremendously!"

At the end of the caroling season, the proceeds were divided equally among all of us including our leader Vising. We would insist on giving her more but she declined because she said we did all the dancing and singing. Since we were three participants in the family, we got the biggest share. My only brother would beg us for some money and chase us all over the house if we refused. Those were happy times because then we could buy new pairs of shoes and clothes. Sweating it out dancing until our legs and feet hurt, and singing until we got hoarse voices paid off well.

"Oh, poor grandma and your sisters too!" lamented Stephanie. "No, Stephanie, grandma enjoyed herself and the others too. They got a lot of money besides," argued Alexandra, matter of-factly.

During those caroling periods, we would be heading home in the evening crossing town and towards our farmhouse two kilometers away. Our means of lighting our way would be a torch made out of dry coconut leaves tied up together with a kind of pliable vine, we called "sulo". We had no flashlights, as they were expensive.

There was a creek we had to navigate to get to the other side of the narrow road lined with tall shrubs, bamboo and mango trees on either side. We would chatter along the way home to partly dispel the darkness and the stillness all around us. I would hang on tightly to my older sister Mary's skirt to keep up with them. My little feet were slower than theirs even if I carried my wooden slippers (bakya) instead of wearing them. I did not want to lag behind in the dark. Darkness always terrified me.

This particular night was gloomy. Droplets of rain began to fall on our bare heads and our sulo began to flicker as the rain hit it. We quickened our pace, hoping that the rain would not entirely put out our only source of illumination before we reached home. So far we had covered only half the way home. There was only one house along our path and before we could reach it, we had to cross part of the town cemetery. This place always gave us goose bumps. My sister, Esther, the one next to me, would often make pranks when we got to this spot. She would run ahead of us, hide behind a tree and scared us with naughty noises. My Manding Mary used to scold her for making me real scared.

"This is getting a little scary now, grandma!" interjects Alexandra, edging closer to her grandmother. "Do be quiet, Alexandra, let grandma continue," her older sister cuts in. "To me this is getting more interesting," Stephanie adds, also moving closer to the other side of grandma.

"And is getting more scary, mind you," warns grandma. When we were in the middle of the creek, we suddenly heard the bamboos creaking above us as if a strong wind was passing by but there was no wind. It was calm and still. Then, the mango trees lining the path from the creek were shaking and swaying as if some strong arms were pushing them. The thick shrubs were making loud, cracking noises like someone was deliberately breaking their twigs.

My sisters and I ran as fast as we could, terrified by the unexpected happening. Whatever it was, it continued with more intensity as if wanting to scare us to death. In the confusion I lost grip of my sister's skirt. I was the slowest one and so I lagged far behind them. Making things worse, I stumbled and hit my chest on a protruding stone.

I was unable to breath for a while, both from fear and from the impact of the fall on the stone. I seemed to have lost my voice and could not scream for help. Luckily, my other sister Precy, looked back and called my other two sisters who were now well ahead. They half-carried, half-dragged me from the terrifying occurrence without stopping or looking back. We managed to get home in the dark somehow, stumbling, breathing hard, but quiet and steady. We lost our torch in the struggle to get away from the inexplicable happening.

"Heavens Grandma!" the girls gasp, horrified. "What was it? Did you find out exactly?" Stephanie asks incredulously.

"We never found out what it was." Mama said "Engkanto" (supernatural beings), or "multo"(ghosts).

My father said, "Nonsense! I come across that path daily, sometimes in the middle of the night and nothing bothered me."

Mama persisted saying that several people had similar experiences particularly during moonless and rainy nights. Nobody however, had seen what and how they looked like.

From that time on, we never stayed in town beyond twilight time, unless we had our father or our brother with us. We sought another way back home from town too. We avoided that shortcut route particularly during night times and followed a wider, cleared road although it was two times the distance to our farmhouse.

V

HOLY WEEK AND EASTER EVENTS

HOLY WEEK IS THE MOST revered of all events in our town. "What is 'revered', please grandma?" Stephanie asks, pen and paper in hand. "Venerated, most respected."

During this season, people would go to church everyday and pray, do the Stations of the Cross, go to confession, observe fasting and do good works, etc, pretty much like what Catholics do here in the U.S. and in other Catholic places. My mother would prohibit us from laughing and enjoying ourselves because we were not supposed to be happy when the Lord is suffering.

A practice unique in some places in the country, most notably in Quiapo, Manila is a sacrifice done by some men. They were called "flagellants". This involves the flagging of the participants as they carry the cross on their shoulders barefooted and without shirts, along the streets, a re-enactment of the Way of the Cross-by Jesus Christ. This is still practised to this day.

"I have seen this at one scene of a movie, you know, grandma. I pitied the men who were flagged with thin ropes," Stephanie joins in. "What is flagging, Stephanie?" Alexandra asks, "whipping, to punish," grandma gives the answer, putting her arm around the younger granddaughter.

Another practice unique to our town is the imitation of the Resurrection of the Lord on Easter Sunday. Every year, the Church Committee would choose a small girl who could sing to act as an angel, announcing the resurrection of Jesus from the tomb. I was chosen from a group of ten candidates as the angel. "You probably looked like an angel too, grandma," says Alexandra.

A procession of two groups, one comprising of only men, and the other of only women, would go on opposite directions and meet in front of the church where a platform stood. The two groups would carry on their shoulders statues of the Blessed Virgin, the Patron Saint of the town, and other statues. The statue of the Blessed Virgin would be deposited on a covered table in the middle of a platform outside the church while the other statues were returned in their places inside the church. Throughout the procession, the crowd of people, usually most town folk led by the church choir would be singing hymns with the accompaniment of the band. My father was the head of the band. He played the saxophone while the other members played other wind instruments.

"Excuse me, grandma, were all the people in your town Catholics?" a thoughtful question from Stephanie. "No, dear, in fact, in our town, there were many other religious sects but they were overwhelmingly outnumbered by Catholics." And although these rites were done at an unholy hour at four o'clock at dawn, many people would not miss it, including children and older people.

High above the platform where the Blessed Virgin's statue stood surrounded with vases filled with varieties of fresh flowers, a large basket made of woven bamboo hang, suspended with a rope attached to a pole. The little angel (me) sat in the middle of the basket, and at the singing of "Salve Regina" hymn, a man lowered the basket slowly until the angel was on level with the statue.

I was dressed in white sequined gown and on my back was a pair of wings made of white crepe paper and cardboard attached firmly with safety pins. As soon as the angel reached the statue, the band and the singing stopped. It was then expected that the angel would sing as she puts the crown on the Blessed Virgin's head. Everybody was quiet, anticipating the angel's sweet song.

The band and the choir had long stopped but there was no sound from the angel. I was fast asleep! The people looked up and saw the angel with closed eyes! Laughter ensued and the solemnity of the occasion was somehow disturbed. Stephanie laughed so hard rousing her sister from dozing off.

Mama rushed forward and asked that I should be lowered to ground level. She shook me hard from my slumber. When I opened my eyes, I blinked at the glaring lights from the torches and kerosene lamps all around me. They hoisted me back up to the platform where I performed the crowning and the singing. My voice was hoarse and sounded like the croak of a frog, as I was still half asleep.

"He! He! He!" Alexandra's drowsiness is now all gone as she joins her sister's giggles. Grandma cannot help but join in the contagious laughter, recollecting the funny episode.

People were still laughing about the incident after the High Mass that followed the ceremony. When we got home, my older sister pinched me hard on one arm, making me scream.

"Why did you sleep up there? People were laughing at you and my friends were teasing me about it." "Do not blame the child," my father spoke. She could not help herself. I could have slept too, if I were the one up there alone in the cold. They all laughed.

"They will never choose you again as an angel, Nene," my mother said tenderly, stroking my short hair. "No. After tonight, she will not have another chance. Besides, she will be too big for the basket by next year anyway," my eldest sister adds with conviction. I was too sleepy to care.

VI

TOWN FIESTA

AS THE HOLY WEEK WAS a revered and most solemn event in our town during those days and still is today, the town fiesta was a most-awaited and most festive occasion, and is still today too. This event is celebrated on the 4th of Dec. every year. At one point, the townspeople were in disagreement about the day. Some said it should be celebrated on the 3rd, instead of on the 4th. The proponents of the latter ultimately prevailed. In our town, small as it was, there existed many religious sects, from Catholics that comprised the majority, to Protestants, Aglipayans, Jehovah's Witnesses and other denominations. They differ in their ways of worship but as far as fiestas, they seemed to unite in enjoying the festivities. Playground demonstrations, contests in singing, dancing, declamations, etc. drew huge crowds not only from the locals but also from neighboring villages and towns. There were also beauty contests that in reality money contests, because the one who had the most money would win even if the contestant was not necessarily the most beautiful.

My oldest sister Meding put me in the list of candidates for Miss Kid Lopez Jaena. I was about 8 years old, thin and freckled but they said I was very pretty (I don't know). "Grandma," Alexandra tugged at my left arm, "Do you have pictures of yourself when you were still a small girl? May we see them?"

"Sorry girls, I do not have a single picture of myself here, maybe in some place somewhere in my town. I will ask some old friends of my sisters when I visit my town again."

"My opponents were: my neighbor, a classmate in Grade II, 3 other girls from the outskirts of town and the only daughter of the Elementary School Supervisor, Marietta. Although the other contestants came from mostly affluent families, the daughter of the supervisor was the predicted winner because she was not only pretty but they were considered the most well-to do in the community. My father who was the head of the town band objected to my candidacy because we could not compete with people who had money. All six of us, my four sisters and I, and my only brother were in school. My two older sisters were enrolled in a prestigious high school in the capital. My brother was in the Public High school but would demand the highest allowance. My two other older sisters were enrolled in the local Catholic High School. Our incomes from my father's work as policeman and from our coconuts were hardly enough to support all of us. Also, the price of copra fluctuated a lot.

My mother and older sisters would not listen to Papa's objections to my participation in the contest. They sold tickets for my candidacy enthusiastically covering every inch of the town and going as far as the other towns as well. My sisters' friends and suitors also got involved in generating the much- needed cash. "Did you win grandma?" Stephanie asks anxiously.

"Alas, I didn't. Marietta, the daughter of the school supervisor won as predicted. I came in 4th, or the third runner up." "Oh!" the two girls sigh sadly.

"And you know, girls," grandma continues, "I was very young, about eight, but at that age, you could feel humiliated, especially that I had the most simple gown. My mother sewed it from her old white dress. On the other hand, Marietta wore the most beautiful gown, glittering all over with multi-colored sequins, and her consort was the most charming boy you would ever see. Marvin was his name and he was wearing a tuxedo with a red tie on his white long-sleeved shirt. Everybody's eyes were on the handsome pair. How I envied them!"

I felt small and forgotten, walking at the tail of the entourage in my simple gown and ill-fitting shoes. I would stop several times during the parade to adjust my shoes which kept on slipping. It was a hand-me down from my sister. I wished I were somewhere else instead of being there feeling insignificant and ignored. I felt like running away but I persevered. My family would have been shamed if I did.

"Poor grandma! I could almost picture you in that situation," said Stephanie sincerely, while Alexandra looks at grandma with sympathy all over her small face.

I had one consolation, though. When the parade was over, my teacher hugged me and whispered, "You are the prettiest among all of them, you know? I would have selected you as the queen."Maybe she guessed my humiliation and offered some sort of relief.

A few years afterwards, my oldest sister won the title of 'Miss Town Fiesta.' She was then a popular schoolteacher in Baliangao, a few towns from us. She was very pretty, had long, shapely legs, fair skin, which she inherited from our mother, and a figure that young men of the town swoon for. She deserved to win by all counts; especially that she had the backing of the son of the Mayor of Baliangao. He eventually married her in spite of my mother's objections.

He was rumored to be a womanizer. We believed my sister was a big influence as he changed in his ways after marrying her.

He later on inherited his father's political clout and became the town Mayor himself. He turned out to be a good husband and a doting father to his six children. They never missed coming to our town fiestas although they lived in another town far from ours.

VII

LEECHES!

IN THE VALLEY DOWN THE hill where our farmhouse stood, there was a river which flowed from the high mountain miles away. It ran through trees and shrubs, rice and cornfields, huts and farmhouses. In some areas, it was deep and wide, in other parts, shallow and narrow.

In our part of the river, my sisters and I often did our bathing and washing of clothes in it. Our immediate neighbors consisting of 4 families would also do theirs there mostly during Saturday mornings. Shrimps and small freshwater fish abound in the areas where the flow of the current was slow. We would catch them with our bare hands in-between dives into the deeper part of the river.

At times, a farmer would bring his carabao (buffalo-like mammal) to dip into the river on the other side. That side of the river was murky from the wallowing of the animal. When my neighbor-friends and I got tired of frolicking in the water, we would go gathering guavas or catch butterflies along the riverbanks. My sisters always had bundles to wash as we would do the washing only once a week. That meant staying in the area for most of the day to bleach the white clothes in the sun, rinse them and wait for them to dry before heading back home.

I was trying to catch a huge multi-colored butterfly hovering over a guava tree when I lost balance and fell into the muddy water. I couldn't swim well but I was not afraid because the water was only about 2 feet deep. I was 7 years old and that depth was relatively easy for me to wade in. I emerged from the water regretting that I did not catch the butterfly which by now had disappeared into the brush up river.

I joined my friends playing ball with a round dry coconut on a clearing close to the edge of the river.

"Hi! Look! You have leeches on your two legs!" Nenita screamed in horror. When I looked down, indeed there were at least three large leeches on my right leg and four smaller ones on my left. I screamed and screamed while trying frantically to shake off the bloodsuckers. My two older sisters who were busy washing downstream came running to my rescue. My three friends were too horrified to do anything.

"Sit down and rub your legs on the sand," Nang Precy half-shoved me down. My other sister Mary broke some twigs from "handilib-on", a plant with big wide leaves that have very rough texture. She crumpled the leaves and rubbed off the leeches off my legs. They then finished the leeches off by hitting them with stones. Blood sputtered on the ground as my sisters hit them furiously. "Aargh!" Stephanie exclaims.

"Grandma, how do leeches look like?" Alexandra asks curiously. "They look like worms. When they attach themselves to any part of your body they suck your blood. When they are full, they expand in size. The two girls shiver hearing this. I think that nowadays they are used in laboratories. Would you like to hear another leech story?"

Both girls nod enthusiastically, shifting positions on the couch closer to their grandmother.

VIII

MORE ON LEECHES!

"GRANDMA, WE SHOULD LIKE TO hear more stories about leeches," Stephanie speaks as they settle for another story on this Saturday night after they have seen a movie, "Eight Below." Their auntie Bing had told them to see this story about dogs left alone by themselves in Antarctica. "Why the big interest on those loathsome creatures, sweetie?" grandma wants to know.

"Because I just remembered that my teacher in English had assigned us to write an unforgettable or unusual story which we had heard from family or from others. The story has to be about animal or insect encounters." "What about the bees?" Alexandra suggests. "I think bees stories are more common than about them bloodsuckers I would like to write about something not common," her sister replies wisely.

"But of course, I have another leech story," grandma agrees as she settles on her favorite spot on the couch. "This is just a short one. Just as well because it is now half past nine o'clock. Tomorrow, I would like you to be up early because we are going to attend the 10:30 Mass at St. Mary's church. We have been invited to my friend Thelma's 80th Birthday at 12:30 in Sleepy Hollow."

"Grandma, before you start another leech story, may I ask one question? Did you swim at the same spot again where you had the leeches on your legs?"

"No I stayed away from the muddy part of the river that was stagnant. That is where they like to stay, not in clear, running water. Now, for my next leech story."

During the rainy season, the small river that bordered our rice field would be swollen. My sisters and I would descend down the hill towards the area. Our neighbors would also join us. Since we were all young and all girls, we had on underwears only. There were logs lying along the riverbanks. We would use these logs as canoes. The older ones would carry the canoes upriver beyond the rice paddies. Then two or three would get into the canoe and use our hands and feet to paddle the canoe downstream. It was a lot of fun. Our shouts of glee could be heard from a distance. Other children from the other side of the valley would come and beg to join us. Soon, there was a big crowd of revelers enjoying the new kind of sport.

We took turns in boarding the canoe and since I was the smallest, I always was allowed to board in each trip. Finally, when I got tired I disembarked from the makeshift boat and headed to the clearing where my older sisters were roasting young corn. I lingered at the riverbank for a while, splashing water over me and picking water lilies.

While I was walking towards my sister Mary and Meding, they looked at me horrified. "Leeches! You have leeches all over your legs!" they shouted in unison. I screamed and screamed so loud that my mother who was resting at the time came running down the hill towards us stumbling as she did so. My sisters loathed them and were reluctant to do something to remove the suckers from my thighs and legs. There were some on my back too.

Without saying a word, my mama scooped sand from the riverbank and rubbed off the bloodsuckers from all over my body. By then, they had grown fat from sucking my blood. "Aagh!" The girls groan in disgust.

"I would have died of fright!" exclaims the younger girl. "What about your other sisters and friends, grandma? Did they get leeches too?"

"I don't think they did. They did not make a fuss. I think I got them because I lingered at the edge of the river, wading around, and picking lilies that were floating in the water. I stayed too long in the stagnant, muddy water."

My aunt who was a midwife in town told us later to bring salt to rub off them suckers more effectively. Alcohol, she said would even be more potent.

My mother scolded my sisters for not being attentive to their little sister. She was scared to death hearing my frantic cries. She originally thought a snake bit me. I might as well have been, considering the horrible fright those loathsome creatures caused. Even now in my older age, I still loathe them.

I haven't even seen them, but I loathe them too, nevertheless. "Have you seen them, Stephanie?

"No, not actually. I saw pictures of them in the Encyclopedia. They look loathsome all right," Stephanie declares. "Don't have a nightmare tonight," Alexandra, she adds jokingly, as they prepare for bed.

IX

THE ANGRY MOTHER HEN

MY ASSIGNMENT EVERY MORNING IN our farmhouse was to collect eggs from the chicken pens. We had a dozen roosters, two dozen hens and countless chicks that kept on coming. The mother hens kept hatching that I ceased to count how many chicks there were. One day, I stepped on one newly hatched chick. It practically crushed under my wooden slippers, poor thing. I did not see it when I was backing off from a pen.

”Grandma!” The two girls exclaim in a reproachful tone. “Well, I did not mean to step on it. In fact I cried a little but there was nothing I could do. I did not tell Mama about it, for she certainly would have pinched me.” “What did you do with the poor creature, grandma?” Alexandra asks sadly.

"I wrapped it with dried banana leaf and threw it into the garbage pit." Oh no, why did you not bury it, grandma?" Grandma got another rebuke.

"Sweetheart, during those days, a little girl like me would not bother getting a hoe or any other implement to bury a tiny, just hatched chick in the proper way." Grandma puts an arm around Alexandra as she speaks with a hint of apology. "Grandma was right, Alexandra," Stephanie says in grandma's defense. "She was only little. She would not know any better."

After a brief silence, grandma continues. After collecting the eggs, I fed the chickens with dried corn and filled the bamboo tube with water for them to drink. It was a daily routine.

One sunny morning, I was rushing to get my chore done because we were going to the big river east of town for a picnic. It was St. John the Baptist Day. Traditionally, people would go to the seashore, to the river, or to Capayas Island, a tiny island a kilometer from our shore, to have a picnic to celebrate the day which comes on the 24th of June. People would prepare all sorts of food to bring to the picnic. Roast pig or chicken, baskets of cooked rice and root crops, boiled bananas, fresh fruits and other types of food. My mother and our neighbor Aling Juana had agreed to split the preparations. Mama gave her two chickens to roast and asked her husband to pick young coconuts from our coconut grove for "lamaw." This refreshing treat called "lamaw" was prepared by scraping off the meat of the young coconut into a deep container with its juice.

The coconut should be young enough and soft. to be enjoyed. We would then add sugar and milk if available, then mix well. This is very delicious and refreshing, and nutritious too. I loved lamaw, I still do. This was our common refreshment since we had a lot of coconuts.

"Where can we buy young coconut, grandma? I should very much like to taste it. What do you call it again, grandma? Lamaw? What a strange word!" Alexandra says with amusement.

"As I have just said, it is a snack or refreshment prepared from young coconut meat. Ah, yes, they are available at some Filipino and Asian stores. Let's see if we can drop by Edgar's store in West Dundee one day and get some. Sometimes they have it; otherwise, we have to go to Chicago, or to Niles, a long drive from here. Oh, wait a minute. I have been sidetracked. I was going to tell you what happened that early morning while I was gathering the eggs!"

Mama asked me to gather every egg I could find because she was going to make "Torta," a delicious cake, her specialty, for some guests who were coming to the house the following day. I was about to finish my rounds when I noticed that one hen did not join the others who were feeding on the corn. She remained sitting in an old basket looking at me, like she wanted me to go away. I shove and I shove her, but she refused to stand up. Anxious to finish my job, I put my right hand underneath her to collect her eggs with the basket half-full of fresh eggs slung on my left arm.

"EEEK!" The stillness of the early morning was broken by my painful cries. The mother hen was attacking me, picking on my arms, my neck, and was almost all over me if I had not run fast enough. Even then, she ran after me like crazy, causing me to stumble. My basket of eggs fell with me and all but five pieces got broken! I was crying not so much from pain of my bruises but from fear of being reprimanded and pinched by my mother. "Oh dear!" both girls exclaim.

"You should know better than to go near a chicken that is hatching," she scolded me while she examined my bruises. "Come inside the house so we can wash those nasty bruises", she said more gently. I did not get the pinching, probably because of my intense crying from pain, or because she was concerned of my bruises, or maybe both. She picked up what remained of the eggs and covered the broken eggs with soil from a mound nearby.

The picnic was a lot of fun. My three older friends and I swam in the river along with many other children, most of them naked. Now and then, we would get out of the water and grab some food from a makeshift shed. My mother had laid out more food than we could eat: grilled chicken, pork adobo, lots of boiled bananas, rice and fruits. She would call the other children to partake of our food. Both banks of the river were literally occupied with people young and old.

The older children dove into the deeper parts while I stuck to the shallow parts, from up to my waist, to my knee, deep. As I was afraid to swim where the water was over my head, my sister Mary would carry me on her shoulders while she swam back and forth the wide river. My older sisters found some of their peers and swam with them while my brother joined his friends upriver catching fish and grilling them while they were still jumping. My father was the only one missing the fun. He had to work at the municipal hall the whole day. You remember he was a policeman. He had to be on overtime duty that day since the others joined the picnic.

It was almost dusk when we got home from the picnic. Weary from the whole day outing, my sisters and I slept earlier than usual that night without eating supper. I even dreamed I was a swan swimming on a lake, shimmering under the light of a bright full moon.

Then I awoke from a commotion outside our house. Amid the sound of feet running down the stairway and from anxious voices from my parents, I could hear loud cries from the chickens in the pen. But I was so sleepy and tired to care. This happened a couple of times before too. Our fowls were visited and devoured by a snake from the thick bushes bordering our farm. My father had the bushes cleared and burned. The attacks stopped then. Obviously, they were still out there lurking and waiting for the opportunity to strike again.

"Grandma, grandma," Alexandra edges closer, as she does when afraid. Were you not scared of snakes?" "Of course, I was deathly afraid of them but they usually would come out only during the night especially during hot, dark nights. We would always carry torches when we went out at night. These reptiles are scared of light and fire. No one among us had ever been beaten by a snake, thank God!

It was only the following morning when we learned the extent of the havoc that the snake, or snakes had caused. Three of our mother hens were gone. Only their feathers remained, scattered around the pen. And you know what? One of the victims was the mother hen that had attacked me."

"Oh, poor hens!" the girls lament, looking truly disheartened.

X

RICE PLANTING AND
HARVEST SEASON

AT THE SOUTH EDGE OF the farm where a river ran alongside its borders, we had a rice field the size of maybe four baseball fields or so. In the month of June through August when there was plenty of rain, my parents would hire a group of eight to ten people called "hunlos" to plant rice. Two men would prepare the rice paddies for planting by plowing around each paddy. Then water from the river would be diverted into the paddies through a canal to irrigate the field. When the paddies were soft from the irrigation, the hunlos people would prepare the paddies for planting by softening the soil further. Then the seedlings that my father and a helper had previously prepared in a seed bed would be brought in bundles into the paddies on a cart.

It was entertaining to watch the hunlos people take a small bunch of rice seedling with their right hand, plant them in the water-covered soil as they sang in unison. Each movement was accompanied by a certain tune and each man or woman would bend and stretch simultaneously and precisely according to the music they sang. They had a leader who would signal the precise moment to pick up the seedling, bend down to plant and to stretch up and repeat the process over and over again. They all wore wide-brimmed hats and long-sleeved blouse for the women and long-sleeved shirt for the men. They looked dirty and muddy from wading into the knee-deep mud. They did not seem to rest and they did not appear tired.

At midday they would stop to eat lunch prepared by Mama and my sisters usually cooked corn meal, fried fish, salted fish (ginamus) and ripe bananas for dessert. A huge jar of drinking water lay nearby the shed with a big dipper. How they drank! I used to look at them with pity as I watched them eat as if they had not eaten in days! They did not waste time chatting. When they finished lunch, some would lie down on the grass and rest briefly. Others would smoke a pipe or just sat down fanning themselves with their hats until the signal to resume was given. The leader had a small whistle, which gave a shrill sound. I once tried it and gave a wrong signal to the men and women to get up when it was not yet time for them to resume. I got a rebuke from my mother, not a pinch, I was grateful for that.

When the rice was ready for harvesting around October or November, my parents would hire another "hunlos" to do the harvesting. Sometimes we would get the same group of people who did the planting when they were not engaged somewhere else. Planting and harvesting during those days were all done by hand. Modern tools and implements and tractors were still unheard of. As during the planting, the hunlos men and women sang together in unison as they worked. I used to be lulled to sleep from their singing in my comfortable hammock attached on both ends with a rope to an overhanging branch of a huge mango tree.

"Wow! Grandma! I could picture you sleeping soundly in the hammock," says Stephanie, clearly amused. "Did you not do anything to help?" a thoughtful question from Alexandra.

"Oh, yes, I did my little job too. I used to give water to the workers, and each time, I did that, I would get a playful squeeze on my cheeks. That made me proud of myself although the squeezes left mud on my cheeks." The two girls smile, imagining their grandma with soiled cheeks.

One day in early November when most of the rice harvesting were done, my two friends, the daughters of our nearest neighbor and their mother came while my sisters and I were grilling corn in the middle of our cornfield situated next to our rice field. This family was very poor. I knew how very poor they were because they wore the same clothes every day. Their small hut along the river was almost broken down. We would seldom see smoke coming from their kitchen window, a sign that they were not cooking. The family of six could be seen often, gathering guavas that grew wild around the coconut groves or picking mangoes from our farm, or from other farms.

They approached us shyly without saying a word. We invited them to partake of our grilled corn. You should have seen how they gobbled up the food as if they had not eaten in days! "Oh, how sad!" says Stephanie, sounding genuinely sorry. Her younger sister joins in with a low sigh.

"Didn't the father and the mother work?" continues Stephanie. Manong Elias did odd jobs for us and for some families too, only occasionally. Then, he became too ill to do any kind of work. The wife, Manang Etang did some washing for us occasionally only since my older sisters were capable of doing the work themselves. They had a grown-up son who spent his time running around with his peers in town and was of little or no help at all. He eventually eloped with a girl next town. The oldest daughter, my eldest sister's contemporary got married to a schoolteacher from another town, and was giving them help from time to time. I think they lived in hand to mouth existence, so to speak.

We took pity on them, so when Manang Etang asked to allow them to harvest some rice from one of the three paddies that were left out for some reason, we readily gave permission. Unknown to us then, my parents had set aside the three paddies for some special purpose.

A group of three distinguished-looking men called on us the following day. I heard they came from a Rice Research Institute. I did not know what that meant then, and neither did my sisters. They came to see a particular rice crop which was a cross section of two varieties. My mother was then the president of the Women's Club in town and was chosen to plant this special variety in our rice field. Our farm was the closest to the heart of the town, and besides, my parents were quite well known. They were voted to participate in this so-called research.

When the men, my father and my mother went to the rice field, my mother was stunned to see that one paddy; the choicest crop among the three had been harvested! My two sisters and I who followed from a distance recoiled and were about to run, but Mama caught us with "psst!" her usual way of calling us. She beckoned to us to approach with a look that meant we were in big trouble. "Girls, you were here yesterday. Did you see who did this?" No one could speak. We knew pretty well the outcome of our behavior: pinching or lashings with dried coconut midribs.

"Oh, oh," the two girls chuckle at the same time. "Mama looked at each one of us, expecting a speedy answer, and a good one too.

"We did Ma," I volunteered weakly, with my head bowed, unable to bear mama's stern gaze. We allowed Vicenta, my friend and her family to harvest that paddy. They said they were always hungry. We pitied them. Manang Etang said to thank you and papa. "They will not be hungry again in one week poor people," my sister Precy found her courage to speak in a way that she hoped would appease our mother.

Mama was red with anger, and probably with embarrassment too that the men would not see the "special rice variety."

"Don't worry, Mrs. Bongcaron. We will make our report about the two varieties and say that the other one has failed."

That noon after the men had left, Mama called us into the bedroom. We were cowering with fear from the lashings which we knew for certain would follow.

"Grandma," Stephanie cuts in. "That's child abuse! Our teacher says it is punishable by law to beat up children!" Alexandra has a little story to tell too. "My teacher had reported my classmate's mother for beating her up with a handle of a broom when she spilled flour all over their kitchen floor."

"Children, during my time, physical and verbal punishments were common even with grown-up kids. That was how children were brought up and disciplined. Children grew up obedient and straight, as a result. It is a different story nowadays, particularly here in America."

Anyway, we got hit five times each with the whip that hang ready on a hook at the back of our bedroom door. We were also asked to kneel in front of the altar and promise not to do it again.

"Stay kneeling until I tell you to stop", was mama's command. She did not come back until about thirty minutes later. Papa came in with her.

I don't think the children knew about the rice research. They simply took pity on our poor neighbors," he said, looking at his children still kneeling, with pity.

"They should have asked me first," mama countered, still angry. Papa was the kindest, soft spoken and most loving father one could ever wish to have. He never punished or raised his voice for anything that we did. He was my mother's opposite.

"Grandma, do you have pictures of your parents? I should like to see how they looked like," Stephanie inquires. "Yes, I do too," Alexandra reinforces. "Sadly, none, girls. If you remember, I told you before that picture taking was not common then. People did not have cameras those days. To have your picture taken, you had to go to the capital where they had a photography studio. And then, you had to wait days before they were ready. They were very costly too."

I can only describe to you how my parents looked like. My mother was considered one of the most beautiful in her time. She won as Queen during one of their Town Fiestas when she was young. She had long hair, very shapely legs, tall, had fair skin and a figure that all the other girls envied. They said that none of us sisters got her good looks. Only my eldest sister Meding came close. Her father, our grandpa, was half Spanish, half-Filipino. I saw an enlarged picture of him once, at my aunt's house. He looked very handsome. My grandma was a native, but very beautiful too, although to me, she looked a bit plump.

My mother, according to my aunt's stories, had a string of suitors, not only because she was beautiful, but because my grandpa was one of the town officials, well-off and influential. Of all his twelve children, mama was his favorite. That's why when my mother eloped with my father, grandpa was so furious he did not allow them to even go near their big house. His objection to papa was because he was poor, the son of a tailor who migrated from Negros, Occidental, a province across the sea from ours. But papa was a good-looking guy, quiet and well mannered. He was a musician and could play all wind instruments. He taught music to teenagers in town and in the neighboring barrios. But all the same, my grandpa looked down at him because of his humble beginnings. He after all owned vast property, rice fields, coconut groves, farm lands, horses, cows, etc. On the other hand, papa had nothing to boast. But mama loved him although she had well-placed suitors, one of whom was my grandpa's choice for her.

For many years my grandpa had snubbed them. It was only when he was dying when my mama was allowed to come back. I was then newly born. He died soon after mama came back to look after him.

"Did your mother get some of her parents' properties, grandma?" the older granddaughter asks.

"She sure did, of course, each of them twelve brothers and sisters got fair shares. My mama got one rice field, coconut grove, mangroves and a piece of residential property."

"The rice field where the special rice was harvested by your neighbors. Was that from your mother's parents, or from your father's parents?" Stephanie continues to ask. "Oh no, we had sold all of my mother's inherited properties to support us all in school. The farmhouse and the property around it, including the rice field was inherited by my papa from his uncle."

"Grandma, is it possible to go to the place of your childhood and see planting and harvesting of rice?" a surprise question from Alexandra.

"Maybe, just maybe, child, who knows? It is so long ago and far away, as a fairy tale goes. The place could be entirely different now. I may not even recognize it anymore. It was almost 60 ears ago since I left our farm house," grandma says, as she ushers the girls into their bedroom. As grandma turns to leave, Stephanie grabs her hand and blurts out:

"Grandma, did you love your mama? She seemed to have pinched you and punished you a lot." Startled by the question, grandma sits down on the edge of the bed that the two children share, and says solemnly: "We loved our mother very dearly, as we did our father. They did everything to provide and support us, did their best to maintain a happy, healthy family".

We saw how much they sacrificed to send us all to school, much more than the other parents did. Our mother only did occasional pinching, scolding and beating to teach us good conduct and proper behavior. Other parents punished their children in much more severe ways. Anyway, like I said, that was how children were brought up differently during those days. Sometimes we resented those petty punishments. My older sister Mary, I think suffered more than any of us. I saw how much she resented them. She eventually migrated to Manila and got a job there without finishing high school. In my case, I resented the pinchings and scoldings too, but you know what? My mother always compensated us afterwards by being sweet and giving certain concessions. She was by no means all that mean.

In fact, she cared for us so much she sacrificed many things for herself for our sakes.

I will again emphasize that children were brought differently during those days than today. You are lucky to have been born these days and time in so many ways. Now, you go to sleep. It is getting late. We are going to the Prime Outlet Mall tomorrow morning and then go swimming at Stingray Bay in the afternoon," grandma concludes as she kisses both girls goodnight.

XI

THE BEEHIVE

"HAVE YOU SEEN A BEEHIVE? No? Not when you went to Brazil?" grandma asks as she settles in her usual place in the couch. "A beehive is a dwelling for bees, where bees make honey." "Oh yes, I've seen those in a movie," says Stephanie. There must have been thousands of them in that round cluster."

"My story to day is both funny and serious," grandma begins the evening's story, on the second week of the children's vacation.

One late afternoon in the height of summer, I decided to call on my neighbor to go guava picking. Guavas were in abundance around and outside our farm all year round and particularly during the summer. They grew wildly in all parts of the town. Every backyard had guavas trees. They were so common that nobody paid attention to them except to pick them to feed the pigs. A song had been written about guavas, and sang when we were in the primary grades. It went this way: "Guavas are ripe! Guavas are ripe," grandma sings briefly. A story about lazy John and the guavas was a favorite tale in children's books in our school library.

"Stephanie, have you tasted guavas?" Alexandra asks her sister. "No, I haven't, but I've seen pictures of them many times in the illustrated books I came across in school. Have you?" Stephanie countered. "No."

"They are of different varieties, some big and round, others, small and oblong, and they are sweet when ripe, and sour and bitter when not, depending on their variety," grandma volunteers information, although not solicited. "But girls, our story is about beehives, not about guavas, remember?" grandma quickly adds before the girls pursue the topic of guavas. "Teach me that song, grandma?" Alexandra pleads.

The sun was just beginning to go down behind the coconut groves and the air was thick with a mixture of varied smells from copra drying up, of ripe jackfruit, and pineapples around and in the back of our farmhouse. The mouth-watering aroma from the kitchen where mama was cooking dinner of boiled chicken with lemon grass did not seem to merge with the other smells. An excellent cook, she prided herself with turning the simplest dishes to fancy fares. We would always look forward to meal times. I only had half an hour to wander around before she would call for dinner. I went to our neighbor's house to ask Vicenta to join me romping around. Their house was only about 500 yards from ours. They were our closest neighbors.

My calls were answered by Vicenta's mother who was sewing something on their porch. Vicenta had gone to the seashore to pick seashells. It was low tide and good for gathering shells, and if I hurried, I would probably catch up with her, she said. I declined thinking that my mama would not allow it as it was almost dinner time. I wandered around the house looking for something interesting to do. My sisters went to a choir practice in town with my father who led the band in accompanying the hymns. They were expected home any moment now.

Back at the house, I went around to see my favorite pig, Lino, as I called him. He was fat and looked very healthy. My sister said that Lino was likely to be the one my parents would slaughter during the next Fiesta in our town, six months ahead. "Not if I could prevent it!" I said to myself, as I patted his big rounded face. He made the sweetest "Oink! Oink!" that I felt like hugging him.

Next, I went to the other side of the house to check on the chickens. Most of them had their eyes closed as the sun was now about to set, sleeping time for them. Then I remembered that I spotted a couple of big, shiny guyabanos this morning when I looked through our bedroom window. The guyabano tree was leaning partly on one corner of our house, laden with fruit. When they look shiny, they are now ripe and ready for picking.

"Guyabanos? What in the world are those?" Stephanie asks, amused by the strange word. "They are of the jackfruit family. They also have spikes on their skin like the jackfruit, but their skin is soft, unlike the jackfruit that have tough skin and sharp spikes. They are green even when ripe, and oh, they are so sweet and juicy. They are said to be very nutritious, rich in vitamins, minerals and fiber too. I doubt if you can see them here even in the Asian stores. They are basically tropical fruits. They probably are available in some areas I don't know of.

"The more you tell us these stories, grandma, the more anxious I am to see the place where you were born," Stephanie remarks. "Me too. Wonder if Daddy will allow us to go there one day?" her sister joins in thoughtfully.

"When you are older perhaps. It is a very long journey from here. First, you have to take the plane from O'hare International Airport to China, Japan or South Korea. This will take about eleven hours and a half non-stop flight with any airline going to Asian countries, like Japan Airlines, China, Korean, and Singapore Airlines, etc. Some U.S. and European airlines would fly passengers up to a point in Asia and arrange for connecting flights to the passengers'final destinations. In my case, I usually would have my connections in Seoul, S. Korea if I takeKorean Airlines, Tokyo or Osaka if I take Japan Airlines.as the case maybe. After a stopover of about four or six hours, you take another plane to Manila. This takes around four and a half hours flight, depending which Asian country you originate from. Then you will take another domestic airline to Ozamiz city the capital, or Dipolog, Zamboanga. From there you will take a bus or a car to Lopez Jaena, my hometown, which is approximately one and a half to two hours drive from the airport.

"Oh, wow! It sounds very far indeed! Would you still want to go, Alexandra?" Stephanie asks her younger sister. "Would you?" is the counter question. Grandma looks at each girl then continues:

"I believe your daddy will not allow any of you to go on such a long journey without him, not in the near future anyway. Besides, the place is far different now from when we were still living there. The other year, before your grandma Mary died, she went and visited the place where our farmhouse once stood. The whole area was like a forest, she said. There was not even a trace of the old house. Two old mango trees were looking like they were about to fall. However, surprisingly, the other one was still bearing fruit. Now, where were we in my story? Ah, the beehives!"

grandma soon recollects, as she shifts her position on the couch.

The guyabano tree was laden with so many fruits that it was leaning on one side, many of which looked ripe. I reached out for the ones that were within my grasp and lay them one by one on the grass. There were still three larger ones that were beyond my reach, so I decided to climb the tree, shaking off my wooden slippers, as I did so.

I was about to grab the biggest fruit hanging on the other side of the tree when a swarm of bees attacked me! I did not notice the beehive attached firmly behind the tree trunk. I screamed and screamed while I was trying to fend off the insects. They were all over me, on my arms, legs, neck, even on my face, which I tried to cover with one hand. I slid from the trunk, bruising my thighs and my legs. I fell down on the base of the tree, hitting my head on a shrub, fortunately not on the stone. "Oh, grandma!" the girls gasp, holding their breath.

My mother saw what happened through the kitchen window and rushed with towels to cover her face and mine. She got stung too, but not as badly as I was. We ran from the bees and into the house, where mama wiped my stings with hot towels. She then went out and gathered some medicinal herbs from our garden. She pounded and squeezed the juices from the herbs and applied them on the affected areas of my skin. She was all anxious and comforting, cradling me in her arms, rocking me back and forth as if I were a small baby crying in pain. The hurt from the bees' sting subsided, but I could not eat well during dinner from the trauma. My mama fussed about me and my sisters exempted me from helping clear up the kitchen. We had daily schedule and mine was to help after dinner time. Not tonight. Everybody felt sorry for me.

That night, I was restless from the sting experience. I cried and cried like a baby. My mama cuddled and rocked me again in her arms until I finally slept. The following morning, I cried even more when I saw myself in the mirror. My face was swollen badly and unrecognizable. My eyes were reduced to slits and my ears were as big as the rabbits' ears.

"He! He! He!" the girls laugh heartily. Adding to my misery, my mama forbade me to go to school that day, I hated to miss school even for just one day. I was one of the best in class. Even only a day absence would give my rivals an edge. The thought was hard for me to bear.

"Grandma, my mom, who is a nurse, as you know, said that some people are allergic to bees sting," interrupts Stephanie. "That's true, but I was not allergic obviously. On the second day, the sting marks gradually healed. My mama's herbs helped a lot."

"What happened to the beehives?" the younger granddaughter asks.

"My father built a fire close to the tree. The smoke drove them away. From that time on, I never climbed a tree again without looking around carefully to ensure that there were no beehives attached to it."

XII

A SHAMEFUL TRIP

"WOULD YOU LIKE TO WATCH another movie tonight, or would you prefer to hear another story?" grandma asks her grandchildren after they finished watching "It's a Mad, Mad, World." "Grandma, that movie was so funny I could watch it again next time," declares Alexandra. "But no, I would like to hear another story about your childhood grandma. What about you, Stephanie?" she turns to her sister.

"We only have three days left here. I would like to hear all of grandma's stories before we leave. We can always watch movies but grandma's stories are original and true," says Stephanie with conviction. "We can borrow DVDs from the video stores, but we cannot borrow grandma's stories," she adds matter of factly.

"My story tonight is something I am not very proud of telling, but I will tell it just the same because although it is unpleasant, I would not be very honest if I withheld it from you."

This happened before I went to school, so I probably was four or five years old. As I have mentioned earlier in one of my previous stories, I always insisted on going with mama wherever she went and when she refused to take me, I would cry hard until she relented. And of course I would get a pinch for being such a brat but I did not mind. To tag along with her was such a treat for me then, regardless.

She was bound for the farthest end of our province, south of Misamis Occidental, to a town called Bonifacio, named after one of our national heroes, Andres Bonifacio. To get to the place, we had to cross five towns including Ozamiz City, where the only airport in the province was located. The only means of transportation to get to the place was by bus or by boat. By bus, it would take about six to eight hours, maybe more of very dusty and uncomfortable ride. By boat, it would probably take two to three days on the rough channel.

Mama wanted to visit an ailing aunt who lived in one of the barrios in Bonifacio, and to buy some clothing material in Ozamis on the return journey. "Grandma, I hear the word 'barrio' a couple of times in your stories before. What does the word mean?", an interruption from Stephanie. "A barrio is maybe an equivalent of a village or county here in the United States, more or less.

In my country of origin, a province is composed of several towns and each town has about five to six barrios or more surrounding it. Now, they also have smaller groups called "purok". Each barrio has its own set of local officials who are answerable to the town officials as the town officials are under the jurisdiction of the provincial administration, and so on.

We started waiting for the bus that would come every hour interval at the crack of dawn. I fought hard from sleeping on the bench as my mother threatened to leave me behind if I slept. When it came at last, it was very full, as was always the case. A good gentleman seated at the end of the long, hard wood seat, gave up his seat to my mother. Mama seated me on her lap, not only to save my fare but there was no other vacant seat.

Now and then passengers would get off, but somebody else would board the bus in his or her place. Some men would insist on riding the already overloaded bus, with their bodies hanging outside it precariously. We had heard of stories of people falling from the running buses and getting killed. A local ordinance was passed forbidding people from hanging on the side of buses, and preventing bus owners from overloading their vehicles, but these ordinances fell on deaf ears. The scarcity of buses and increase in the number of passengers moving from one place to another made it hard to stop the dangerous practice.

I was squeezed between a pregnant woman seated next to us with a child on her lap, and a fat man leaning towards us trying to hang on the side of the bus. It was very uncomfortable for me. It was worse when the bus would turn a curb. He would lean more heavily on us when the bus would turn left, and when it turned to the right, the pregnant woman and her two-year old baby would be leaning against us. I was feeling extremely uncomfortable but I dared not complain. After all, I insisted on going with my mother. How I regretted it then!

I have to describe to you girls how buses in my province looked like then. They were not the same type of buses we have here in America, I can tell you. They were open on both sides so that passengers could get in and out on either side of the vehicle. The seats were of hard wood. Only a few had thin cushions on their seats. Most of the buses were old and worn out, and almost always they were overloaded, particularly when they were approaching a big town. Passengers were mostly farmers transporting their products to the next town, or to farther towns where there were open markets. Some other passengers were students and working people.

There were no supermarkets in any of the towns as we have here, so people would go to the open markets on market days, usually once a week, to buy their food needs. The top of the buses were always filled with farm products, such as corn, sweet potatoes, bananas, rice, even pigs and chickens, and other food products, making the top of the bus look like a market stall.

"Wow! What a sight they must have been!" exclaims Stephanie. I could make a funny drawing from your description, grandma."

Whenever the bus would stop to unload or pick up passengers, there would be peddlers hawking all sorts of delicacies: rice cakes (bibingka), banana and corn fritters, boiled corn, roasted peanuts, popsicles, fruits and other stuff. Most of the peddlers were young children. There were also pregnant women carrying basketful of goodies, and old men and women, thin and haggard begging passengers to buy their foodstuff.

I was sleeping most of the time in spite of all the discomforts and noise from the roar of the bus' engine and from the passengers, calling the peddlers and bargaining hard with them. My mother bought some stuff for me, and pretty soon, I found myself digging into my mother's bag, munching this and that. I insisted on buying more roasted peanuts and popsicles despite my mama's protests. Before we got into the third town, I was so full I fell asleep again. This time, there were vacant seats since some of the passengers had gotten off at the capital. I could now lie down fully, with my head on my mother's lap.

Halfway to the next town, I awoke with pain in my belly. I sat up, feeling I should go. The bus was running fast and it appeared no passengers were either getting off or boarding the bus anytime soon. I desperately wanted to ease myself that very instant! I tried to call the attention of my mother but she appeared asleep. And then the inevitable happened!

"What? Grandma?" the girls ask alarmed. "I did it right there in my underwear! It made a swishy sound too, as it came out beyond my control. People near us began to smell it, and their 'Oh, whoa!' awoke my mother. She begged the driver to please stop, which the man did with some reluctance. She then yanked me off the vehicle and half-carried me into the bush along the road. There, she cleaned me with crumpled leaves of some soft plant in plain sight of everybody. Some people suppressed their laughter but the children in the bus hollered. Even the driver could not help himself."

A kind elderly lady offered to clean up the mess left on the bus seat with some crumpled newspaper moistened with water she carried with her. My mama finished cleaning me up with a moistened face towel she always carried in her bag. She appeared visibly upset but calm.

"Ha! Ha! Ha!" the girls roar in laughter. Alexandra covers her nose with her hand as if she smells the foul odor. "Oh, grandma, that was gross!" says Stephanie still laughing. "You know, what?" grandma continues. I did it again on the return journey! I ate a lot of roasted peanuts and boiled corn again. Good that it was already dark and we were stopped at the bus station when it happened the second time. I was at the entrance to the restroom when it started coming out. I tried to hold it but it came slipping down my legs. She really pinched me hard this time out of frustration." You are not coming with me next time, girl, she said indignantly."

XIII

FIESTA HAPPENINGS

"GIRLS, I HAVE ANOTHER STORY about fiesta or festival as it is commonly called here. I should tell you this story because the one I told you before did not include other interesting happenings which are hard for me to forget even to this day."

"Grandma, please do. Our days in your house are numbered and it will be a year before we can come here again," implores Alexandra. And next summer, you may not be here. You said you will be on a cruise again, Stephanie puts in. Where will you be going next year, grandma?"

"Yes, that's right. I plan to go to Northern Europe. I had been to so many countries in that continent but I haven't visited Ireland, Scotland, Iceland, Greenland and

London, England. I will make my reservations with either Norwegian Cruise Line or Princess Cruise Line; whichever is offering a better deal. And by the way, my next series will be about my travel experiences. I hope your cousin Gabriella will be with you then. Your half sister, Olivia who is three years old will still be too small to enjoy storytelling, and Brian, your only male cousin is still a baby."

"Buddy, Tinsel, move. Look at how these two are crowding me on the couch," Alexandra complains as she pushes each of the sleeping dogs. Tinsel jumps out of the couch and settles on the recliner, while Buddy remains stubbornly in his spot.

"We shall have avocado ice cream which I made before you came, after my story", grandma says as she settles down across Alexandra and Buddy on the other side of Stephanie on the larger couch. "Show me how to make avocado ice cream, grandma", Stephanie asks. "Sure. We have to make a trip to Walmart or to Caputo Supermarket on Randall Rd. to get avocados and other stuff. I have other business in that section of Huntley also.

"Like I mentioned in my previous story about Town Fiesta, this event was a very special and much-awaited day in my life. It is still today, mind you. The celebrations would last for a couple of days, starting with a Solemn High Mass and then followed by activities put up by students and staff of St. Francis Xavier High School, named after our Patron saint, St. Francis. By the way, St. Francis Xavier is our well-loved patron. It was believed that during the height of the Muslim Pirates' invasions in our province and in neighboring provinces, a miracle happened. Other towns were invaded and robbed by the pirates but our town was spared. Some fishermen claimed that they would see a very tall, lean man patrolling our seashores during the night. The man was wearing a long, white robe and was seen with his hand outstretched towards the sea, as if stopping something. And in the morning, the church cleaners would notice that the Saint's robe was filled with amorsicos, like the Saint had been out in the field wading through the grass. The townspeople believed that the man seen on the beach was St. Francis Xavier, protecting the town from the invaders."

"Wow! Did you believe that story, grandma?" Alexandra inquires. "I did, of course. Other people believed in it fervently, including my whole family".

"Hmm, amorsicos," I don't think I heard that word before," Stephanie's mind was on something else. "Amorsicos are kind of tall, slender grass with blades. They have seeds which stick to your clothes if you wade through them. They grow abundantly in warm tropical climate. I haven't seen them anywhere else, here or in other countries I had been to."

To continue my story, our fiestas were, and are still dedicated to St. Francis Xavier. The public elementary school would put playground demonstration contests, participated by contingents from the barrios. It was a lot of fun watching the colorful costumes worn by the contestants in the dance and calisthenics contests. My class in the fifth grade once won in the dance contest, accompanied by my father's band. His band always featured in all town and church activities, as there was no other source of music accompaniments. There were no DJ's like we have today.

I used to go with my elder sisters to the ballroom dancing held at the municipal hall in the evening concluding the fiesta. I would sleep under one of the corner tables after I got tired watching my older sisters do the waltz, rhumba, boogie, cha cha, and tango. My middle sister Precy was the star dancer. How she could dance the night away! She was very pretty, with slim waistline, shoulder length curly hair, and smooth fair skin, like my mother's, though not as tall as mama. She was very much sought after by the young boys in town.

On the other hand, Esther, the one next to me, was a very good singer. They said she had the voice of Carmen Rosales, the popular singer at the time in Manila. My other two older sisters were beautiful too and had many admirers. My only brother Benjamin Santiago, was a good saxophone player. He was tall and handsome, like one of my uncles on my mother's side. The girls used to swoon at him, even after he got married to his childhood sweetheart. My parents were mighty proud of their children. I could tell even in my young age.

"What about you grandma? Where they proud of you too?" Not during my younger age. I was freckled, thin, naughty, and was a cry baby. But they said I had my mother's profile. When I was in high school, I won in a very tight declamation contest."

"Declamation? What kind of a contest was that?" Alexandra wants to know. It is reciting a poem with action. You had to be very distinct in reciting every word of the poem and demonstrate or act what you say. My topic was "Curfew Must Not Ring Tonight." My English teacher from Cebu, Miss Siervo coached me well. It was about a man accused of betrayal during the French revolution. He was doomed to be executed at the ringing of the curfew bells. His lover did all she could to save her sweetheart. She encountered extreme difficulties, endangering her own life, but she eventually saved him from the gallows." Curfew did not ring that night that could have signaled the man's death. Many wept while I did my declamation, which I did with all I'd got.

"Bravo, grandma!" the girls cheer. Your family must have been very proud of you!"

"There were many more activities in our town fiesta that I am not able to tell tonight. But how we all enjoyed them and looked forward to every fiesta day! However, there was one fiesta I really was sad. Remember Lino, my favorite pig? Well, my sister's prediction came true. They slaughtered him when I was not around to protect him. I was in town doing an errand for my mother. Perhaps I was sent away purposely so that I would not witness the sad event. I cried the whole night, refusing to eat dinner until my mama threatened to whip me."

"Poor Lino!" the two girls look as sad as their grandma. She continues after a brief pause.

"Anyway, during fiestas, guests went from house to house to enjoy the food. Every household prepared special food, and people just came uninvited. That was the practice. Although our house was off the center of the town, many guests would skip the other houses and go to our house. I think my mother's popularity as an excellent cook spread. They would come from other places out of town, and the gentlemen came not only for the fine food, but also to get a glimpse of my older sisters and seek acquaintance with them."

During one fiesta day, a big typhoon came. The guests who came in the morning or during the course of the day could not go home. Strong winds and heavy rains swept and battered our house throughout the day. Our house was made of wood and of corrugated iron and nipa roofing. It shook and felt like it would be uprooted from its foundations. Everybody got nervous.

The storm raged on until dawn. It dissipated slowly and stopped completely by mid morning the following day. Our guests did not have a choice but remain in our house. We only had three bedrooms, one larger than the two others. We had a dozen guests who stayed the night. Our living room, our porch and even part of the kitchen were used as sleeping quarters. All my sisters slept in the larger bedroom, while I slept with my father and mother in the smallest room. I had no idea where my brother slept that night. He materialized during breakfast, looking like he did not sleep at all. My poor mother, assisted by my older sisters, never seemed to rest from preparing meals and serving them to more than a dozen people.

That was one fiesta I would never forget. First, I lost my beloved pig Lino and then the typhoon which was the strongest I ever yet experienced. Part of our roof was torn off, many of our crops and trees got destroyed and one of our dogs disappeared. Our chicken pen broke down and many newly hatched chicks died from the cold.

When my father checked our farm north of the house, he came back looking sad. Many banana trees and young coconut plants got uprooted. Two fallen coconut trees blocked the path to our house. Many other trees, especially those that were planted on the slopes fell down. Luckily, numerous coconut and mango trees surrounded our house, so it was shielded from the brunt of the storm. Also, it was neither planting nor harvesting season for rice and corn, and our coconuts had been harvested, dried and sold before the fiesta. The devastation would have been worse for us.

I was too young to worry about crops and trees. I was still mourning for Lino, although my father gave me a cute, three-months' old piglet, which I named Lina, Lino's replacement. He said the chances of her getting slaughtered for future fiestas was nil because of her sex. She most likely would be used for breeding. That gave me some consolation.

But I was still unhappy because the storm prevented us from watching an open-air movie in town. The movie was "Gongadin." There was no movie house in our town, or the adjacent town of Plaridel, for that matter. To watch a movie in a theatre, we had to take a bus to the capital some 14 kilometers away on a rugged, dusty road for an hour or so. The only theatre in the capital was always too full. My sister or my mother had to lift me up to be able to watch the show. They had to stand in the back of other people when the seats were full, and would take turns in holding me up to be on level with people's shoulders.

The open-air movies were most anticipated in our small town but they were scarce. From time to time, some advertisement shows would come along, like ads for detergents and soaps, cooking oil and such, but they too would come only occasionally. The real shows would be during fiestas for two or three nights only, and would not come again until the next year's fiesta. We hardly had any other entertainment. There was no television, no radio, no malls, and other amenities you girls have today.

"What a time and place to live, grandma?" Stephanie says sadly. "Yes indeed! You girls are very lucky to be in this age, time and place. But we did not know any better," she adds, smiling at the girls, as she heads towards the kitchen to get the avocado ice cream.

XIV

MEMORABLE MAY

"GIRLS, THERE WAS ONE RELIGIOUS practice which children from age 5 to 12 years old in our town really looked forward to every year, which was done during the month of May", grandma says to the girls after supper one evening. "It is still practiced today, but maybe not as elaborate and as interesting as we did then. It is called "Flores de Mayo", or in English, "Flowers of May." We probably inherited it from the Spaniards who, as I have mentioned briefly somewhere in some of my previous tales, colonized the Philippines for three hundred years. We had been colonized by many other countries, but the Spaniards' influence on our culture were many, and remain even to this day, such as religion, food, our love for music and dancing, and many other ways of living, social, moral as well as spiritual."

"Grandma, this sounds like history, isn't it? Explain "colonize" to me please," the older grandkid requests. "Why, I thought that the word is simple enough for you. You are in Grade V, aren't you? Anyway, to colonize means to settle, to establish, as in to come and settle in a country and establish or form a government or society, for an indefinite period of time." Now, may I continue? When both girls nod, grandma clears her throat and resumes.

"Ah, before I go on with the Flores de Mayo story, let me just mention an event that made the month of May more memorable for me. This happened on the first day of May.

I was awakened very early that day by my mother's anxious, but hushed voice, talking to my father. "Crispin", that was my father's name, by the way, and my mother's name was Isidra. When my father did not answer, she shook him and repeated, "Crispin, there is a young lady sleeping on the sofa. My father sat up surprised and said, "What?" "Wonder who she might be, and why she is here."

From where I was lying on the other side of the room in my single, rattan bed, I could sense my parents' agitation. I continued to listen, pretending to be still asleep. "What should we do?" My mother went out again and peered into the living room once more. Just then, I heard my brother's voice: "Ma, come here, please. Is papa awake yet?" Hearing his son's voice, papa went out of the bedroom and they all headed to the kitchen. I did not hear them anymore but I could no longer go back to sleep, wondering what it was all about. Later that day, the news became clear to everyone in the household. My brother had eloped with one of his girlfriends. "Grandma, grandma," Stephanie tugs at grandma's arm. I heard that word "elope" before, but I do not quite understand what the word really means.

Elope means to run off secretly, with the intention of marrying. Anyway, my parents did not waste time going to the girl's parents' home and discuss their intention to have the two lovers joined in marriage in the earliest possible time. Those days, it was a disgrace to live together without the benefit of marriage. Both parents were devout Catholics and adhered strictly to their religious's traditions.

Papa and mama gave the girl's parents the dowry. I didn't know how much. "Dowry" is either money, piece of land, or something of substantial value that the woman or her parents would offer to the groom or his parents before the marriage took place," grandma explains before any of the girls could ask her to explain the word. The more well-off any or both the parties are, the higher or the more pricey would be the dowry. Being the only boy in the family, I Believe my parents put up a lot.

And so, the wedding date was set, and almost immediately, the preparations began. Our two biggest pigs and several chickens were lined up for the big feast. It was the usual practice to have a large feast we called "kumbira", after the wedding ceremony, which involved not only big expense, but too much fanfare and jubilant celebration, where all the town folk came, invited or not.

I was the flower girl and my three sisters were the bridesmaids. My father's band provided all the music during the high mass and all through the wedding feast. Everybody seemed happy and having a great time, except my brother, the groom, for some reason. He looked to me like he was distracted and a little sad. I could only surmise he did not want to get married. He was only twenty years old then.

A few months later, when my new sister in-law was six months pregnant, my brother disappeared. He took off to an undisclosed location. None of his closest friends in town could tell us where he went. Nang Oding, his wife, was left devastated, naturally. We gave her all our sympathy and support, but she remained unhappy. After his son, (our first nephew) was born, she appeared better, but she decided later on to move to a relative's place very far from our town. I guess she wanted to forget her sad fate. I heard much later that she found herself a boyfriend and got married again.

"Do you girls have any questions before I move on?" Grandma sounds like a teacher asking a question to her pupils. "Ah, yes, grandma", Stephanie raises her hand slightly. You have mentioned your father's band a couple of times. What instruments did they play?" Oh, they had the wind instruments: saxophones, trombones, clarinets, trumpets, percussion instruments like the drum and cymbals, also string instruments like guitars and banjos. Somebody also played the harmonica. "Hmm! Wish I could have seen them!" Alexandra remarks wistfully.

"Have you seen those old Italian movies wherein the band would follow the bridal entourage from the wedding ceremony in the church, to the reception, playing their music during the festivities." "What happened to your brother, grandma? Did you ever find him?" Stephanie's next questions.

A couple of years after he left, we heard he settled in Cagayan de Oro City, in another province north east from us. He married a beautiful girl of half-Spanish blood, or "mestiza." He had six children with her. He died about six years ago of a stroke.

Now, I think we are ready for my next May event, "Flores de Mayo, yes?" "Yes. Yes, grandma. It sounds interesting," both girls agree. Alexandra positions herself opposite her grandma on the other side of the living room couch so that she can stretch herself. Her older sister remains at grandma's side with the two dogs at her feet.

Like I said, before, "Flores de Mayo" means "Flowers of May", so called because flowers were so much a part of the event. Every afternoon, about 4:00 p.m. throughout the month of May, girls, their mothers, relatives and friends would gather in the church to attend the Flores de Mayo. This is started with a Novena to the Blessed Virgin, followed by the saying of the Holy Rosary.

Then, a group of 8 girls dressed in white would go to the altar one by one, where the Blessed Virgin's statue stood on a white linen-covered table. Each girl would carry a letter from the prayer "Ave Maria", so the first girl would be bearing the letter A, the next V, and so on, until the whole eight-letter prayer were installed on a bench holes, in front of the statue. While the procession of each girl was in progress, the people would be singing the Hail Mary. This was followed by the offering of the flowers to the Blessed Virgin. All the children would then go to the altar and place flowers around the Blessed Mother. Then, the children would go around the statue and toss flower petals to the Blessed mother. All this time the choir continued to sing hymns, until all the flowers had been offered and all the participants were back in their seats. It was a beautiful ceremony, and the children just loved doing it.

My sisters and I never missed a single day attending the Flores de Mayo. Our problem was, the scarcity of flowers. When all the children in town roam around town each day to pick flowers from gardens, backyards and even from the bushes for one month, you could just imagine how scarce the flowers had become. Our own garden became bare of even buds before the middle of month.

One day, on one of our jaunts to hunt for flowers, we passed by a house with a large flowering tree growing in the front yard, filled with pink blossoms. The yard was fenced with bamboo about six feet high, but the blossoms were drooping over part of the fence. My older sister Mary decided that we pick some of the blooms, the ones drooping outside the fence. We helped ourselves, but Manding Mary wanted to pick more. "Nene, come. Let me hoist you up. Reach out for more flowers. I can't get to that big bunch in the back," she said to me, and carried me up.

I was cutting off the bunch starting with the largest one, and was poised to cut the smaller one, when a large, black dog suddenly appeared from somewhere in the house. It barked so loud that I lost grip of a branch I was holding onto, and I fell on the ground next to my sister, on a pile of dried coconut leaves. She held me anxiously and was about to run half-dragging me, when the fence door was flung open and an elderly man peered out.

He was just about to let the dog after us when an elderly woman, obviously his wife cried out, "Gomer, come, come, dog!" She shoved the ferocious animal inside the fence, then beckoned to us to come back. We reluctantly retraced our steps, expecting to be scolded by the woman. The husband went back inside the house with a scowl. My other sister had fled ahead of us.

"Next time girls, you just ask. There's more than enough flowers for everyone of you. You are Manong Crispin's daughters, aren't you?, she said kindly. Come back here again next time."

We went off happily with more flowers than we hoped to pick that day. It was only when we got home that I be felt pain on both my knees and on my left arm. I grazed them on the bamboo fence as I fell. My mother as usual fussed over me and would have scolded my sister had she not sought sanctuary somewhere in the back of the house.

When I told the story to my father he said, "Oh, that was Amparo. She knows me and your mother. She used to come here to barter fish with our crops years ago."

"I used to give her some of my preserved pineapples and jackfruit too", my mother re-enforced my father's information.

"That was a memorable May, indeed, grandma. I could clearly see you, picking the flowers and then falling," Stephanie says smiling. "I will draw grandma hanging there, with the black dog barking at her", the younger girls joins her sister, grinning widely.

XV

SOME SCARY TALES

"I HAVE A FEW SHORT episodes to relate tonight," grandma says, as they are finishing clearing up the kitchen after dinner on Sunday night. These stories are a bit scary.

"Oh, Stephanie will love that. She is fond of horror stories, aren't you Stephanie?" Alexandra gives her sister a slight shove on her arm. "Watch out! You almost knocked down the plate I am wiping!"

"Yes I like scary stories, grandma. In fact, I have most of Harry Potter's series. I only need a few more to complete my collection."

"Alright, then, finish up and follow me into the living room," says grandma as she lowers the kitchen blinds and heads to the living area.

A. The Mad Dog

Dogs roamed freely in our towns and in neighboring areas. They were not kept in cages or kennels. They were never on leash. Owners would call them during their feeding times and give them food in their feeding bowls outside the house. They were not allowed to stay inside the house or to sleep with them in their beds. During rainy days which were frequent during the Southwest monsoon season in the months of July up to December, the dogs would take shelter under the house or in some cases in the doghouse. People in our part of the world during those times did not care about their pets as much as we do here in America.

I do not know of any animal hospital in our town or in our province for that matter. When a pet was sick, it just died without having been given any chance of a cure. Some unscrupulous people would even kill them for food or maltreat them with beatings or kicking, whatever. The poor animals were an unhappy lot, I guess. But we did not know or practice any better. It was a general practice to treat them dogs or cats in inhumane ways. In our case, we did not show too much affection to our dogs and cats as we do here, but we did not maltreat them either.

"Poor pets!" the two girls comment. "Didn't someone get fined or imprisoned for being cruel?" Stephanie inquires. "No, we did not have any "Cruelty to Animals" laws, like what we have here in America," grandma replies, petting Tinsel as Buddy looks on." I do not know now.

What I'm telling you now may not be true any longer. This happened decades ago, you see." This time, she also pets Buddy.

"So dogs as I have said, would wander around seeking food as they were always underfed. Their owners would feed themselves first before thinking about their dogs. You could see them walking around looking thin and sickly, poor things. When I see dogs here being pampered and treated like human beings, I lament for those poor animals during my days.

Grandma stands and sits between Tinsel and Buddy sleeping peacefully in their places on the couch. She puts her arms around each lovingly. "You lucky creatures!" she says, rubbing their furs. Tinsel groans lowly, as if to say, "Yes, indeed!" Buddy jumps and scratches his fur around the ears, then settles close to grandma's feet. She goes on :

Some dogs got sick and violent, particularly during the height of the hot season in March and April. They would growl at anyone who came near them, and bite. They were usually rabid and since there were no available rabies vaccines then, people who were bitten got sick too. I heard of a child attacked by a rabid dog. She died three days afterwards. Other similar incidents happened elsewhere, so my mother strictly forbade us to go out to town and other places without a stick, in case we would encounter a mad dog. The mad dogs were particularly violent when it was very hot in the middle of the day.

One early afternoon after lunch, my two sisters and I decided to go picking blackberries (lumboy). My mother was resting and we dared not make noise while she did her 'siesta.' The other day, my sister Esther got pinched hard on her ears because we were noisy playing jumping rope in the yard near her bedroom.

We set out riding in a cart drawn by our carabao (like a buffalo). Sister Mary was riding on the animal's back, guiding him while Insi Esther and I settled in the cart. When the carabao sped up with my sister's whipping, I got thrown off the cart, as I was not holding tight on the shallow cart's side. I landed on a heap of dried grass. Meanwhile, my sister kept on driving the cart until my other sister hollered hard to stop her.

Sister Mary jumped off and ran towards me anxiously, forgetting to secure the animal. As a result, the carabao ran off with its screaming passenger. My sister caught up with it in time somehow, before it went down into a muddy pool. I was hurting a bit, but not bad enough to cause any crying. I was lucky, I did not hit a stone or a lying log, or something hard.

"Oh dear! What a start to an outing!" Stephanie comments. Alexandra chuckles with her.

My sister tied up the carabao securely to a coconut trunk nearby and climbed the first row of berry trees that was laden with ripe, purple fruits. My other sister followed behind her. I was asked to stay beneath the tree to pick up the berries that fell on the ground. They had a small basket each to put the berries in, and when they could not reach the berries that were on the outer branches, they would shake the branches off. The ripe berries would then fall into the ground. My business was to pick up the fallen berries and put them in my little basket.

Suddenly, I was halted from my work with my sister Mary's loud, anxious voice: "Nene, Nene! Mad Dog! Mad dog!" She was frantically calling me while sliding off the tree trunk. She then picked me up and pushed me up the tree to the nearest branch, and hoisted herself up the tree close to me.

Looking down below, I saw what my sister was agitated about. A very thin, brown dog, with its tail drawn in, was hovering around the tree. Its nasty teeth were bared. It appeared very hungry and was looking around for something to eat. Although we were safely up the tree, high enough for him even if he would jump, I shivered with fear. We were all very afraid.

115

For some reason, the dog did not show any sign of leaving. It remained there, munching the berries that were on the ground and then it lay down on the grass close to the trunk of the tree, as if waiting for us to come down.

We were in a very uncomfortable position. My sister Mary and I hugged together on a tree branch not big enough to sit on a prolonged period of time. She would not dare move to another branch, afraid I would fall if she left me. My other sister was higher above us, perched on a branch and hugging the tree trunk, like a bear, afraid but more comfortable.

We remained in that predicament for about thirty minutes or so, wishing we were elsewhere instead. I became pretty restless, but my sister would not even allow me to lower my feet down the branch from our crouched position.

Just then, we heard whistling. Two men were coming from the other side of our farm.

"Manong Jose! Manong Inteng!" my sister called out to the men who were about to turn around a bend on the narrow pathway. She knew them as workers in our farm. "There's a mad dog! Watch out!" she hollered, pointing down the tree. The two men grabbed dried coconut branches and shooed the animal away. When it showed resistance, Manong Inteng, the bigger and younger of the two men pulled out his bolo (sundang), getting ready to strike in case the mad dog would attack. It walked slowly away at first, and then sped up when the men threatened to strike it.

"That was some experience, grandma," Alexandra exclaims putting her small hand over her mouth. "Whew!" was all Stephanie can say with a sigh of relief.

B. Witch Story

There were a lot of weird happenings in our town, some of which are hardly credible today. One of those is about witches. During the Lent season we called "Cuaresma," rumors usually spread that some people had encounters with witches. These encounters normally would happen in remote places where there hardly was anyone around, and would take place during the middle of the day when it was very hot, or during the late dark evenings.

One rumor had it that a lone man was coming home from a far barrio one late, moonless night. He was coming from serenading his ladylove. Now, during those days, serenading was a very common way of courting a girl. One person or a group of persons, all men, would go to the house of a girl, the object of attention on a designated night with guitars or accordion, or saxophone, whatever instrument they could play well. They would sing and play their instrument in front of the girl's house for a couple of hours, depending on whether they would get some attention from the girl and her family. If the parents of the girl liked the suitor, they would invite the serenaders into the house and let them continue their singing inside. Sometimes, the girl's parents would serve them snacks and drinks. This meant encouragement to continue the wooing and subsequently engagement, if the parties love each other. It is a practice we got from the Spanish, who ruled our country for three hundred years. One day, I shall tell you the great influence the Spaniards had on our culture, one of which was the practice of serenading.

Back to the witch story, the man was walking along a shallow river path with a dim flashlight, his guitar slung over one shoulder. He was about to cross the creek when suddenly a woman wearing a black robe blocked his path. The woman had very long hair that almost touched her ankles, and was smiling wickedly at him. The witch started to dance in front of him with her hair swirling around her like they were blown by some wind. Startled, the man wheeled around to look for a stick or any weapon for he was sure this was a witch. Unable to find one, he took his guitar from his shoulder and struck the woman's ugly face with it as hard as he could. The force was so hard it broke. He heard the witch's shrill cry that seemed to echo beyond the stretch of trees and brush across the valley. Then before he could blink, the woman disappeared as quickly and as silently as she came. A loud sound like flapping wings of a huge bird made the man fall on his knees in fear. He swore to his friends later on that he did not make up his story.

"How scary!" Alexandra covers her face with her hands, as she usually does when scared or sad. "Grandma, I like that story. Was that really a true happening?", asks Stephanie.

"As much as I know, dear. My father and my mother never allowed us to go into town or elsewhere alone, even during the daytime. We heard of a similar incident happening uptown, which up to now, baffles me. Again, this was a woman with long hair who appeared to a boy, about twelve years old, on a deserted road during the middle of the day."

The woman according to the boy, started dancing in front of him, practically blocking his way. While the witch was dancing, her long hair was getting into the boy's ears, mouth and covering his eyes. The boy was choking, but fortunately he managed to run as fast as his legs could carry him away from the dancing witch. In the distance, he spotted a man on a carabao coming in his direction. He screamed. The man got off the animal and held him before he could stumble on the road. When the boy looked back, the witch was gone. The man took him to his home in his carabao, still trembling with fear.

"My, Oh, my!" Alexandra mumbles, edging closer to her grandma. "What stories! I certainly have not heard or read stories like them! I will relate them to my friends in school who also like scary stories," declares the older girl, who does not appear scared at all.

"Maybe you can include these stories in your writings in the future, elaborate and expand them. Perhaps you will come up with interesting fiction with these tales," grandma pats her older granddaughter's hand. "Do you wish to hear more scary tales?"

"Yes, yes, please, grandma. It is only fifteen past nine o'clock. One more, please." The two girls beg.

My Grand Uncle's Magic Powers

My grandfather from my mother's side had several brothers and sisters. Like I mentioned in my earlier stories, they were of half Filipino and half-Spanish blood. They were all good looking I was told, with fair skin, long pointed nose, and taller than their native counterparts. What I was not told though was how many they were. Perhaps they had died or had moved to other places. My mother did not tell me about all of them. I never came to know any of them except my grandfather's youngest brother. He was tall and handsome and had many girlfriends. He looked very similar to my grandfather in the picture. I saw my grandfather only in his picture for as I told you before, he died when I was newly born.

Papa Juancho would often come to our house and play with my sisters and me. Sometimes he would bring some lemon candies and throw them on the ground. He loved watching us scramble for the candies scattered on the ground and among the grass. Usually, I would cry because I was not as quick as my bigger sisters and would get only a few of the candies. He would then fish for more candies inside his pants pocket and give them all to me. I would stick my tongue out to my sisters who later on would woe me for some of the candies.

Papa Juancho was known to possess magical powers. He could speak some Latin. We had no idea how or where he learned it. During those days, Latin was used in Masses. It was considered a very powerful medium of communication, and prayers said in Latin were regarded as very effective.

It was common during those days to hold séances, gatherings wherein a leader or spiritualist attempts to communicate with spirits. A group of people would sit around a round table, meditate, put their hands flat on the table or hold hands. The leader would then start calling the name of a dead friend or relative. The group would sense the spiritual presence by the candle being blown off even if there was no wind, or thumping or tapping could be heard in the room. "Oh, oh, oh!" the girls move closer to their grandma.

My grand uncle would often be a leader in these kinds of gatherings. He would also perform some kind of magic and was regarded as very smart and knowledgeable in many things.

He claimed to have seen a lot of apparitions or spiritual encounters. Some of his stories included battling enchanted creatures. One night, he said, he was coming home from a far barrio courting a beautiful daughter of a rich landowner. It was very late and gloomy, with light showers, the kind of night one would prefer to stay home and curl up on a couch. He had only a small torch, which would flicker in the light rain now and then.

When he was crossing a small wooden bridge, a loud thump in front of him startled him. When he looked up in the semi-darkness, he saw a very large, tall man towering above him with hairy skin and bulging eyes. His arms were as big as posts and his legs as large as coconut tree trunks. He was towering high above granduncle that he could not make out his face. He froze for one second. This was a wicked giant, he thought, starting to feel afraid. But his fighting spirit prevailed. Without wasting another second, he recited a Latin prayer. Lo and behold, the giant fell on his back over the bridge and into the creek below. The fall created a loud, crashing noise. The giant let out a blood-curdling cry that would have scared an ordinary man out of his wits. But my uncle stood his ground. He continued to recite his Latin prayer without pausing or running, until he reached home.

A similar happening occurred that mama had related to us. He was on his way to town, one early evening on an errand. He decided to take a quicker way to town by taking his boat, instead of walking to town. Their house was situated along a large rice field, and across the field was a wide river where his boat was moored. He would use it for fishing and for transportation to the edge of the town.

He was rowing his boat peacefully and smoothly, when he felt that the other end of the boat was tilting, as if someone or something heavy was on it. He felt himself lifted up slightly with the weight on the other end. In the gathering darkness, he could make out the outline of a weird-looking man sitting at the other end of the boat. The man had oversized head and large, glaring set of bulging eyes, like small flashlights.

He stopped rowing, put his paddle aside, then recited his Latin prayers, with hands clasped and his face turned heavenwards. Almost instantly, the weird man fell off the boat. Grand uncle Juancho almost toppled over from the sudden movement. The creature disappeared into the water, as suddenly as it had appeared. He resumed his rowing to the edge of the town, whistling, as if nothing happened.

"Wow! Unbelievable happenings! And how scary too!" Alexandra exclaims. "And your grand uncle was indeed a very brave man, grandma," Stephanie comments, visibly impressed.

My grand uncle Juancho had many more unusual encounters. He claimed to have seen long-dead people, dwarfs and enchanted beings, which ordinary folks did not see. They said he had a special gift. While others did not believe him, many others did. His parents, brothers and sisters believed him one hundred percent. They said he would never lie about anything.

"Did you believe in his stories, grandma?" the girls' last question before they settle for the night. "We all did," says grandma, as she kisses the two good night.

XVI

CONCLUDING STORY

"GRANDMA, LET ME HELP YOU set the table for dinner," Alexandra offers. "Hmm! Smells so good! What is it?," Stephanie asks from behind her grandma. "It's Chicken Adobo, your mom's favorite."

"Oh, I should have watched you cook it." "Well, it's done. You were so engrossed reading your book, I did not want to bother you. Don't worry, we shall cook this recipe again when your father comes the day after tomorrow to pick you up. Look up the recipe among the recipe cards I gave you. The ones we cooked together, do you think you can prepare them on your own when you get back to your Dad's? The gelatin dessert, fruit salad, plantain fritters, the simple dishes: Hamburger patties, Fried chicken, pickled fish, and also Egg salad, Macaroni Salad, Pasta with Broccoli Rabe, yes?" Grandma eyes her older granddaughter with anticipation.

"Grandma, I think I can," Stephanie says uncertainly. "Wow! Stephanie, Mom will be really proud of you," Alexandra compliments her sister smiling.

"Grandma has been a very good teacher," she declares, putting an arm around her grandmother fondly.

"You have been a very attentive student and I want you to continue your interest in food preparation and cooking. It is a skill girls should acquire, and skill in any kind of work can only be developed through constant practice."

"Grandma, do you have another story to tell us tonight?" Alexandra cuts off grandma's next sentence.

"Have you done all the homework your daddy wanted you to do?" grandma counters." I have been doing mine every night before dinner. I do not know with Stephanie."

"I still have two sets of questions in Math to do. I will finish them tomorrow evening before or after dinner," says the older sister.

"Grandma, please, one more story tonight, yes?" The younger girl pleads. Her grandma nods while she settles at the head of the dinner table. "Get on with your dinner and help me clear up afterwards."

"My story tonight is a bit longer than the others. We should be in bed by 9:30 as I plan to go to Spring Hill Mall tomorrow to pick up more stuff for you to take home. I also want to get something for your mom."

"Yeah! Yeah!" the girls exclaim enthusiastically.

"The story I am going to tell you tonight is about lots of fun, as well as a happening that my sisters and I would not ever forget. Well, my older sisters have all died now. I am the lone survivor in our family. Sad, isn't it? Grandma says this, with teary eyes. The two girls look at her with sympathy.

Stranded at Sea!

Going to the seashore to pick shellfish during low tide was a favorite pastime for children and adults alike in my town, which was bordered by shallow shoreline. The whole of my province, Misamis Occidental, is situated along the coast, running through stretches of mangroves and stony beaches.

Low tide would usually occur during the week of the full moon. People would flock to the shores where the seawater had receded, exposing the dry sand and jotting rocks. They would gather whatever they could find from the dried up stretch of land such as, sea shells of different varieties, crabs, sea urchins, seaweeds, shrimps and shallow water fishes. The seashells varied in color, shape and size.

They could either be boiled or grilled. The sea urchins were cooked in the same way, but they could also be eaten raw.

"What are sea urchins, grandma?" an interruption from Stephanie.

"They are rounded seashells with spikes all around them. You could be pricked if you are not careful picking them. It has soft, delicious meat inside. Sometimes the meat inside is full and luscious when mature, other times, you would hardly find any meat inside, when they are young and not ready for picking. We could not tell which was which, so we just picked them at random."

"How I missed breaking them with a heavy knife and scooping the meat with a spoon and eat them raw, with boiled saba bananas!" The girls stare at her in wonderment. "Let me tell you, I am missing so many things in my childhood days," she continues, pausing now and then to reflect.

Picking seashells was a lot of fun, and at the end of each outing from the sea, we would head home with basketful of various kinds of seashells. My mama would cook them right away, as they wouldn't keep fresh. They were particularly delicious when cooked while they were still alive

The clams, the seashells we called "aninikad" and "liswe," sea weeds, some urchins and crabs were easier to find in the dry parts, but more sea urchins, shrimps and fish were usually found in areas that were farther out in the shallow waters among the corrals. You needed a boat to go farther out into the sea with nets and spear to get a better catch. When my father was not working and would go with us, we would go home with more seafood.

Since many people do shell picking and fishing on regular basis, seafood became more scarce. We would go to the seashore early, sometimes at the crack of dawn to beat the others who had the same purpose. When it was full moon, the low tide stretched to about two to three kilometers offshore and would last longer. We would bring food provisions like boiled sweet potatoes and bananas and water. We would eat sitting on the dry sand or on jotting rocks. We would break open the sea urchins and ate our food with bare hands.

"Gosh! Grandma, you ate with bare, dirty hands?" Alexandra's observation.

"Well, there were always patches of water around where the sand had been dug up to find clams," grandma defended her actions. We always washed our hands before eating.

"How did you eat the sea urchins? Did you not say they were full of spikes?" the older girl recalls.

"We would break them horizontally with a kitchen knife which we always had with us, then scoop the meat with our bare fingers into the mouth, as simple as that. Mind you, were they delicious! Um! Um!" grandma emphasizes as the girls watch her with amusement. "Let me get on with my story. We are getting to the most interesting part yet." She makes sure she gets all the girls' attention.

One very early morning, my two older sisters and our two neighbor friends and I set out to go shell gathering. We had asked permission from our father to allow us to use our boat moored at one corner of the seashore near Manong Julio's hut. He was the one looking after our boat, which he would use for his own fishing occasionally. It was big enough to carry five to six people at a time. My sisters and our older neighbor could row expertly. I never learned to row as well as they did.

Since the tide was only beginning to recede, the water was still deep enough for the boat to get through. They paddled until we reached the area where we could see people wading into the shallow water, a sign that the tide was getting low. Farther up where the ground was higher, we could see more people doing their business of shell gathering. My sister Mary dropped us off where the water was now but ankle deep, and she headed to the other side to secure the boat with a rope on a protruding rock. A couple of boats were also secured on the same spot.

We started gathering whatever we could get our hands on that we thought were edible. I found some clams partly hidden in the sand. I knew exactly where they were in the sand where the left zigzag marks on the surface. Now and then, I could hear my mates holler when they would find bigger shells called "liswe," a very delicious seashell, with firm, gummy meat inside. Once, I almost stepped on a large urchin, half-buried among the seaweeds. I was not spiked because we all had our rubber slippers on. My mother would not let us go shell gathering without them, along with our provisions and tools.

When we got hungry, we would dig into our basket of provisions and eat while we continued our task. Most times, we did not want to stop and waste time since the tide did not stay stationary. In a couple of hours, the water would begin to rise again. My sister had warned me and the others to stay close and not wander away from her. We would frolic and splash water at each other in-between looking for more seashells. On the other hand, my sister Mary met a classmate, and they chattered noisily together while busy with the business of shell picking, until the girl left with her cousin.

At one point, we decided we would have a contest of who would fill her basket with shells first. Now, this was not easy for me, being the smallest in our group. I had the smallest basket, but yet, I found it hard to fill it. My two sisters would put some of their finds into my basket to help me win over our neighbors. Now and again, we would hear somebody shout triumphantly that she found big shells, a crab, or urchins, and that her basket was filling up.

I found a medium size crab but it clipped me so I shook it off. It landed a few feet away. Juanita retrieved it in no time, removed its claws and dropped it into her basket. Then we came upon a space between two small rocks filled with smaller shells called "aninikad." We almost bumped our heads picking them in a frenzy.

"Aninikad" are smaller than "liswe." They look identical, and are both delicious, but it is harder to get the meat out of the aninikad shell. We had to use a safety pin to pull out their meat. Of course we had to boil them until their meat were partly exposed,. Then it was easier to get their meat off. My older sister used to take off the shell's meat for me. Sometimes, I would fall asleep in the middle of the meal while I was waiting for her to give me the extracted shell meat.

"Grandma, you slept during meal time?" Alexandra asks smiling. "I often did, and as I did so, my lips would be moving up and down, as if I were sucking a milk bottle. When my mother saw me doing this, she would pinch me awake. She believed it was going to bring bad luck. The pinching woke me up all right, and then I would realize that everybody had finished eating supper." Hearing this, the girls laugh heartily. Grandma laughs with them, remembering that scene in her childhood.

"We were very superstitious those days, particularly my mother. My father would sometimes disagree with her and they would argue for a while. Mama would always prevail, of course. Some of the superstitions she told us and encouraged us to believe were credible during those days but they may sound silly nowadays. I shall tell you some of them next time."

"I got sidetracked again!" Grandma realizes she has forgotten where she had left off. "You and your friends were having a contest picking the most seashells," Alexandra reminds her. "No, Alexandra, grandma was telling about this aninikad, and some other shell," her older sister disagrees.

"Let me see." Grandma ponders for a while then says, "Stephanie is right, Alexandra, but let me go back to when we were still gathering seashells, and trying to get the most yield."

My basket was only half-filled when my sister Mary called out from a distance trying to find out where we were exactly in the crowd of shell-gatherers. There must had been close to a dozen people, adult and children scattered all over the large patch of dry land, maybe a mile or so from the seashore. Rocks jutted over the mounds of dry sand. More people would flock to these areas because usually there were fish and shrimps between them where the water was shallow. There were also more seaweed where it was not dry completely.

Towards midday, the water started to rise slowly covering the mounds of sand, and the jutting rocks and stones began to look like they were trying to hide from view. While a few minutes ago we were walking on dry sand, the water was now ankle deep, a signal it was time to stop our hunt for shells. We surveyed our baskets reluctantly and prepared to leave. Juanita had the most filled basket, but we did not have the chance to compliment her. When we looked up to the horizon where a few minutes ago were littered with humanity, we saw only a few, wading in knee-deep water.

"Esther, Juanita, Lina, Nene, everybody, let's go!" my sister Mary called out from behind us. "Hurry!" she prodded more urgently. "Oh no! Where's our boat?" she asked, almost screaming. We all panicked. The four of us huddled together, holding each other while sister Mary was half-running and half-stumbling on the now over the knee-deep water.

"Our boat is gone! It was there a while ago," she pointed to her left. Maybe somebody stole it, or gone adrift!" she moaned. I began to cry. Sister Esther hugged me closer to her. Lina and Juanita began to cry too, while sister Mary was flailing her hands helplessly. By this time, the water was already my waist deep.

Then we heard rowing from behind us. "Look, somebody is coming!" my sister Esther said excitedly. We all turned and saw a man wearing a wide-brimmed hat, cruising alongside us on a slender but long boat. My sister Mary did not waste time informing him of our misfortune.

"Please, could you help us find our boat? Or could you take us back to shore?" she pleaded. The man pointed to a distance and said, "I saw a boat painted blue out there. Could that be your boat? It was drifting aimlessly in the current."

"Oh yes, that is our boat all right," my sister said with relief. "Come aboard. Let us turn around and try to catch it before it drifts farther away', the man said. The current is getting stronger." Turning to us, he said, "You girls stay right here. I can not take you all in this tiny boat." The man gave my sister an extra oar and they both sped back to where the boat was last seen. While they were gone, the rising water had reached my chest, being the shortest. Sister Esther held me tight with her right hand and the baskets with her left. The other two clung to us nervously while we waited for the man and my sister. By now, we were shivering not so much from the cold, for it was now the middle of the day, and the sun was beating on our bare heads, but rather from anxiety. In what seemed forever, we saw two boats coming in our direction, one manned by the unknown guy, and the other by my sister. He had tied up our boat to his boat with a rope to make sure my sister's boat did not drift away with the current from the rising tide.

"The man saved your lives, grandma," Stephanie says, leaning on her grandma's shoulders.

"Yes, indeed!" His name was Bernardo and he told us he was one of the church choir members. He knew my father very well, and was with him and his band during choir practice every Saturday evening. He spoke well of my father. He said he was a very patient music teacher. He even taught him how to play the saxophone and the clarinet.

When my father learned of the incident, he invited him to have dinner with us on a Sunday evening. When he left, my mother insisted that he brought along a ripe jackfruit, a fattened chicken and a small bag of cassavas, which he accepted with unending thanks.

"Can you describe a cassava, grandma?" Stephanie does not let any word she does not fully comprehend pass without explanation.

"It is a kind of root crop. The cassava tree is slender, with soft stem and grows to about five to six ft. high. The cassava roots are long and look like short spears, and have thick brown skin. You have to peel off or pare the skin to reveal white, starchy meat. They serve a lot of purposes. We boil them and eat them like any other starchy food. We would also grate them and mix with sugar, eggs, and coconut milk to make cassava cakes or fritters. We used to dry some of the grated cassavas that we could not use right away for future use.

The dried cassavas make good steamed cakes, we called "balanghoy." To make balanghoy, we would mix the dried grated cassava with brown sugar and fresh, sliced young coconut and steam them. We would also use freshly grated cassava, squeeze off the juice, mix with grated young coconut, baking powder white sugar and make "puto, or steamed cassava cake." We would use the juice for starching our clothes. So you see how versatile the cassavas are?"

"Versatile?" Stephanie raises her eyebrows. "Versatile means has many uses or purposes, or can be turned from one to the other."

"I should like to see these root crops. Can we buy them at the supermarket?" Alexandra breaks her silence. "Oh yes, they are available at our supermarkets here. I don't know if they are in Miami. Let us get them at Caputo or Meijers on our last food shopping before you leave and make cassava cake."

Going back to Bernardo, he went home that night struggling with the stuff mama gave him. But my story does not end there. He took fancy to my older sister Precy, fourth from the oldest. He came back one evening with a group of young men friends bringing guitars. They serenaded my sister and courted her relentlessly but alas, my sister liked someone else from the next town, an instructor at the capital's best college. Disheartened, he moved to a farther town in Calamba.

We learned later on that he met a schoolteacher and became betrothed to her. My father gave one of our fattest pigs for his wedding banquet. He also offered his band to play at his wedding ceremony for free but he declined politely. His well-off uncle had hired the most popular band from Negros Occidental, named "Island Swing." My father used to go all the way to that province to hear that band play and would bring home music pieces for his own band.

As for my friends, my sisters and I, who were stranded at sea that day, Bernardo was a real life hero. We could not stop relating the story about our vanishing boat to everyone who would care to listen. I even wrote that story for my report in school, "An Unforgettable Experience."

"All right girls, that's the last of my childhood stories for now. It is getting late. Tomorrow is going to be a busy day. We are going food shopping and then prepare a really good dinner for your daddy. Our dessert will be cassava cake (Bibingka)."

"I will make another dessert, a surprise one," declares Stephanie. "I will help you and grandma. Stephanie," says her sister enthusiastically.

"Grandma, wait, there is one question I should like to ask." Stephanie catches her grandma's arm as the latter rises from the couch. "How did you remember all those stories when you said you were still very young, as young as three or four years old in some of your stories?"

"My mother related most of them, and some I heard from my older sisters, still some from my aunts. You are really smart, Stephanie. You ask intelligent questions," grandma says holding both the girl's hands. "And that is not to say you are not smart too, Alexandra," she adds turning to the younger granddaughter. "Both of you are not only pretty but smart, a very good combination. Your daddy should be very proud of you, so am I," she concludes, putting her arms around each girl's shoulders as they troop into the bedroom. Alexandra and Stephanie cling to their grandma feeling sad that they will soon be leaving.

XVII

GOODBYE, GRANDMA

AS THE GIRLS ARE GETTING ready for bed, grandma remembers something. "Girls, next time you come, you will hear stories about my travels to many different places. Africa, Europe, Southern Mexico, the Carribbean Islands, South America, Hawaii, Bermuda, The Middle East, Canada, Alaska, some countries in Asia, in Australia and within the United States."

"Wow! Grandma, you had been to all the continents?" Alexandra sits up in bed looking incredulous. "How very interesting! I can't wait to listen to stories about those places!"

"But grandma, what about stories when you were in high school and when you were in college?" another of Stephanie's smart questions.

There isn't much I can tell when I was in high school. The only episodes I cannot really forget are when I could not attend some of the periodic tests because we owed money to the school. I would usually cry to my heart's content because I did not want to miss any of the tests. I was one of the top in the class and also the class treasurer. My classmates would look for me to get my signature in the test clearances but I would hide at home pretending to be sick. How I hated those times! As I mentioned in my stories, there were six of us in school at the same time and my parents were really hard up coping with all the school expenses.

Our situation eased a bit when my brother got assigned in South Korea, working with "PEPTOK", meaning "Philippine Expeditionary Force to Korea." As a veteran of World War II, he was recruited to work there for one year. He would send us monthly allotment for a period of one year. He paid for most of our school expenses.

A couple of boys in my class were chasing me around in school but I did not like any of them. I had a crush on the school principal who was much older than I, but his interest was on my older sister, the school librarian. And yes, I participated in many school activities, contests in singing, dancing and declamation. I told you about the declamation that I won in my previous story, didn't I?

I have written a novel about my life as a college student, as a married woman with young children, and a teacher, employed as an Education Officer in Nigeria, West Africa. It is an interesting novel, a family drama, most of which truly happened.

"Oh grandma, so you are a writer? I probably took my writing ambition from you?" Stephanie comments happily.

"Not a published writer yet, but an aspiring one," says grandma making a signal to be quiet. Alexandra is now snoring on the other side of the bed. She kisses both girls on the forehead then goes out of the room quietly with the two dogs following her to the back door. They need to be let out before she retires every night, a routine she never fails to do, rain, shine, or snow.

At 6:00 p.m. the following day, as Clyde is getting off his car parked in front of his mother's home, his two daughters run outside to meet him.

"Daddy, you are just in time for dinner!" Stephanie says hugging his father.

"And we have a surprise for you!" says Alexandra taking his other arm and hugging him.

"Where's Angela, son?" his mom asks as Clyde gives her a light kiss on the cheek.

"She is tired, She was on duty last night, and was called again at noon today. There was a premature delivery and the other pediatrician supposed to handle the case begged to be off due to family emergency."

"Oh doctors! Nurses! I feel sorry for them. Their time is not theirs anymore! Your Ate Bing has the same irregular duties at her hospital's ICU. Sometimes she is on call during the day and then goes on duty again during her night shift. I would never get used to missing sleep," grandma declares as she gets busy putting the steaming Nigerian beef stew on individual serving plates. It is one of her son's favorite dishes.

Taking her place at the table she says to her son, "This stew has only very mild spice, not the real Nigerian stew. The children won't be able to eat very spicy food, neither can I. My stomach can not take spicy stuff anymore."

"What's the surprise, girls?" Clyde did not get an answer. The two girls had gone to the kitchen. It is now time for dessert. Their grandma is smiling to herself and says, "Your girls had been very busy throughout their two weeks with me, helping with chores, particularly in the cooking. Lets see what they are preparing for dessert.

Just then, the two came to the dining room with a tray each. Handing one dessert bowl to her daddy, Stephanie declares, "Here's your surprise, daddy!" Clyde surveys the bowl in front of him with a chuckle. "Oh my! This looks

like a real treat!" On the bowl are diced fresh fruits topped with white cream with bits of colored sugar sprinkled on top. Diced red cherries are arranged on the very center of the mound.

"I bet you will not be able to eat your favorite Leche Flan dessert after eating that, son," his mom comments laughing.

"I made the cream myself," Stephanie says proudly. "And I helped dice the fruits!" Alexandra adds smiling widely, showing a deep dimple on her left cheek.

"I am really proud of you girls! I am indeed surprised! Make this treat for Angela too."

"Goodbye, grandma!" The two girls hug their grandma tightly and long, as they are preparing to leave. Her son looks on and then gives her mom a loving kiss on the cheek.

"See you next time, mom." Let's move on, girls", he prods. Your auntie Bing and uncle Ariel are waiting for you."

Alone again after the children had left with their father, grandma feels like crying. Loneliness fills her like heavy chains weighing in her heart. She seeks comfort hugging her two dogs. They seem to feel her misery. Tinsel and Buddy follow her around as if trying to fill the void the two girls' departure with their father has created.

The next summer when the girls are expected to come again seems a decade long. What is she going to do in the meantime, occupies grandma's mind as she turns and tosses in her bed.